What
Lead

"I know of no on~~e~~ ~~..~~~~.~~~~.p~~ than Dr. Jim Bradford. I've watched his life closely for almost three decades. He is a leader I would gladly follow anywhere. His perspective on leadership will take you to a new level of spiritual excellence."

—**Dr. George O. Wood**, general superintendent, The General Council of the Assemblies of God

"Dr. Bradford is a powerful example of a leader whose heart is after God's and whose gifts challenge us to a higher level of life and leadership. From my point of view, his life is in perfect harmony with the teachings of this book."

—**Clarence St. John**, district superintendent, The Minnesota District Council of the Assemblies of God; executive presbyter, The General Council of the Assemblies of God

"I have the utmost respect for Jim Bradford. It is ironic. For a person who has never sought followers, he has become a leader of leaders. Not unlike Joseph, no matter the adversity, he emerges with greater responsibility and opportunity to influence. I appreciate Jim sharing his insecurities about leading and the challenges that leading have presented to him. His authenticity is a breath of fresh air on the subject. It is my prayer that this book becomes a voice for a new generation of leaders—leaders who care as much about the goals of their followers as their own aspirations. Perhaps the highest compliment I could give Jim is that early in my career I trusted my personal goals and aspirations with him."

—**Dr. Chip Espinoza**, author of *Millennials@Work, Achieve Greatness at Work* and *Managing the Millennials*

"Having observed Dr. Jim Bradford's grasp of spiritual leadership, *Lead So Others Can Follow* is born out of his own pastoral experience. This book hits the right concepts in a practical, yet deeply spiritual manner and proves a credible resource for pastors and lay leaders alike!"

—**Jeff Peterson**, senior pastor, Central Assembly of God, Springfield, Missouri

"Dr. Jim Bradford spent three days with me and my leadership team teaching some of the principles in this book. It was life-changing for me and a strategic step forward for our church. Jim is practical, relevant, and approachable. *Lead So Others Can Follow* is a great book to study as an individual leader, but an even better tool for your entire leadership team to study together!"

—**Rod Loy**, pastor of First Assembly of God, North Little Rock, Arkansas; author of *Three Questions, Immediate Obedience,* and *After the Honeymoon.*

"In this book, Jim Bradford has captured the essence of church leadership, addressing the issues of practical leadership/management principles while keeping a focus on the priority of the leader's spiritual vitality. Dealing with these principles in twelve chapters under four specific categories, *Lead So Others Can Follow* is an instructional guide and devotional book that should become a part of every church leader's library. It will inspire and encourage readers to reexamine and strive to improve their leadership roles."

—**Efraim Espinoza**, director, Office of Hispanic Relations, The General Council of the Assemblies of God

"If I could choose an author to write on spiritual leadership, I can't imagine anyone I'd recommend more highly than Dr. Jim Bradford. With the flood of books being published on leadership, *Lead So Others Can Follow* merits our attention. The focus on *spiritual* leadership is refreshingly practical and modeled by a leader among leaders who has practiced spiritual servant leadership over his lifetime. For busy ministers with a heart to lead spiritually in a world of uncharted change, this book rises to the top of my list."

—**Dr. Elizabeth (Beth) Grant**, executive presbyter of The General Council of the Assemblies of God and cofounder of Project Rescue

LEAD SO OTHERS CAN FOLLOW

12 PRACTICES AND PRINCIPLES FOR MINISTRY

James T. Bradford

Lead So Others Can Follow

Copyright © 2015 by James T. Bradford

ALL RIGHTS RESERVED

Published by Salubris Resources
1445 N. Boonville Ave.
Springfield, Missouri 65802

www.salubrisresources.com

No portion of this book may be reproduced, stored in a retrieval system, or transmitted in any form or by any means—electronic, mechanical, photocopy, recording, or any other—except for brief quotations in printed reviews, without the prior written permission of the publisher.

Cover design by Sheepish
Interior design by Tom Shumaker

Produced with the assistance of Livingstone, the Publishing Services Division of Barton-Veerman Company. Project staff includes: Bruce Barton, Ashley Taylor and Tom Shumaker.

Unless otherwise specified, Scripture quotations used in this book are taken from the 2011 edition of the Holy Bible, New International Version®. NIV®. Copyright © 1973, 1978, 1984, 2011 by Biblica, Inc. ™ Used by permission of Zondervan. All rights reserved worldwide.www.zondervan.com. The "NIV" and "New International Version" are trademarks registered in the United States Patent and Trademark Office by Biblica, Inc.™

ISBN: 978-1-68067-073-8

18 17 16 15 • 1 2 3 4

Printed in the United States of America

*In appreciation of
your friendship and service
Enjoy
Roy*

Dedicated to the memory of my father,
Ted Bradford,
a remarkable lay ministry leader,
now with Jesus.

CONTENTS

Foreword 9
Introduction 11

Section 1: Spirituality and Servanthood

Chapter 1: Core Commitments 15
Chapter 2: A Spiritual Center 25
Chapter 3: A Serving Identity 35

Section 2: Systems and Strategies

Chapter 4: Oversight Roles 47
Chapter 5: Strategic Process 57
Chapter 6: Staffing Criteria 67

Section 3: Skills and Strengths

Chapter 7: Team Building 79
Chapter 8: Public Speaking 89
Chapter 9: Change Management 99

Section 4: Stamina and Stability

Chapter 10: Physical Health 111
Chapter 11: Emotional Resilience 119
Chapter 12: Prevailing Prayer 129

Endnotes 138
Acknowledgements 140
About the Author 143

FOREWORD

Jim Bradford has been a colleague for more than twenty years. I first knew him as our family's pastor in Southern California. I learned very quickly that Jim's insights into Scripture and his pastoral wisdom were always rooted in a deep spirituality. His personal life was bathed in prayer, and as he stood in the pulpit or did pastoral ministry, it was self-evident: Jim Bradford had been with God.

His Spirit-empowered life is complemented by a keen mind. He really is a rocket scientist with all the degrees to validate the claim. Reading quantum physics for leisure is not my idea of fun, but Jim's keen mind combs through information in the scientific world and offers insights that few pastoral leaders can glean so effectively. In a secular society, where data rules, Jim Bradford can see the forest through the trees.

While Jim says that *Lead So Others Can Follow* is not a text book, complicated book, program, or secular book, it *is* a substantial volume that all pastoral leaders should take seriously. What you will gain are insights on how a true servant has navigated his call to serve Jesus Christ. The useable practices and principles he offers have been forged in the crucible of real life. The messiness, pain, joy, and satisfaction of following Jesus, as a ministerial leader, yields a transferable benefit for all who will dare to read this book.

Lead So Others Can Follow frames the ministry of leadership for the church around the foundational center of vibrant spirituality. This book acknowledges that organizational systems and strategies must be linked to a leader's strengths and skills. If a vast majority of all deaths, among pastoral leaders, are cardio-vascular related, then the section on caring for one's own physical and emotional health is not to be taken lightly. Finally, don't overlook the simple fact that the final chapter is entitled Prevailing Prayer.

This theme's placement in the final chapter provides the most obvious reason why Jim is qualified to write a book entitled *Lead So Others Can Follow*. I would expect nothing less from my friend and pastor Jim Bradford.

—**Byron Klaus**, president of The Assemblies of God Theological Seminary

INTRODUCTION

For a number of years I lived near the Southern California coastline where the climate is idyllic most of the time. I used to like describing the weather in terms of what it was *not*—not hot, not cold, not cloudy, not windy, and not humid. Or, as a friend of mine would say, "It's just another boring day in paradise."

Because so much has been written on leadership, let me also try to describe this book in terms of what it is *not*.

- *It's not a textbook.* My focus is on the practical and specific rather than the theoretical and general. This is a book designed for people who are actively involved in ministry leadership as pastors or key volunteers.

- *It's not a complicated book.* Each of the twelve chapters has a singular focus and is written to be easily followed and digested. In fact, this book could serve well as a one-chapter-a-month resource for leadership teams to discuss and apply.

- *It's not a program book.* Instead of advocating for specific ministry programs or curricula ideas, the focus is on developing a sustainable, replicable philosophy of ministry leadership that is Christ-honoring and people-centered.

- *It's not a secular book.* Secular management books may reflect biblical leadership principles, such as servant leadership, but this book is about *spiritual* leadership. One of our great challenges as ministry leaders, and one of my personal passions, is to keep our spirituality hard-wired into our leadership.

The book is organized into four sections: spirituality, strategies, skills, and stamina. Each section contains an introductory reflection, followed by three chapters that focus on a leadership topic relevant to that section. I have structured the chapters around a hand-picked set of principles and practices that grew out of my thirty years of pastoral ministry.

All of this is written with a realization that the spiritual climate in our world is changing, especially in the western world. Christianity's center of gravity has shifted largely to the Global South. Many churches in the West seem lethargic, increasingly powerless against the stiff headwinds of cultural secularism, religious pluralism, moral relativism, and aggressive atheism. Meanwhile, spiritual hunger runs rampant in the culture.

Either these are the shadows of death or they foreshadow one more spiritual awakening before Christ returns. Should Jesus choose to delay His coming, I am believing for the latter—both in the West and in the yet unreached regions of our world.

At the heart of such a revival will be ministry leaders who, like King David, lead with both their hearts and their hands; godly shepherds who are spiritually trustworthy and personally skilled.

And David shepherded them with integrity of heart;
With skillful hands he led them. (Psalm 78:72)

I'm convinced that our churches are full of people who are hungry for leadership like that. May our heavenly Father make of us Jesus-centered, Spirit-anointed ministry leaders who serve God's people well and make way for sweeping spiritual renewal in the land.

SECTION 1

Spirituality and Servanthood

On the first Sunday as a new pastor at my previous position in Springfield, Missouri, I made five commitments to the congregation...

- To be a spiritual leader
- To be a growing person
- To disappoint them, somehow, sometime
- To build a people-centered, team-based approach to ministry
- To believe with them for the future of Central Assembly

My understanding of servant leadership doesn't make me feel less of a leader. It does, however, obligate me to make commitments to others before I expect them to make commitments to me. To do otherwise fosters a sense of leadership entitlement that puts me and what I think I deserve at the center, eventually alienating the people I most need around me.

Of course, that third commitment—to disappoint them—is

the one that everyone remembered. Such is human nature. But I reminded them on that first Sunday that there would probably be moments when they, too, would disappoint me. We just needed to face it, get over it, and move on together. And although some people seemed to take perverse delight in reminding me whenever I was, indeed, "keeping my third commitment," there was generally an underlying trust still there—in part because I was not *demanding* that trust but rather had placed myself in a position to *earn* it through the commitments I took responsibility to make.

This is the foundation of spiritual leadership—walking in the Spirit's life, making and keeping life commitments, earning trust, demanding little for ourselves, and lifting others up.

CHAPTER 1

Core Commitments

"Watch your life and doctrine closely."
1 TIMOTHY 4:16

As a kid I was short, shy, and definitely not the dominant personality on the playground. By the time I was off to college, the thought of being a leader was terrifying to me. But that fear, as with many fears, turned out to mean nothing. After years of open doors and stretching experiences, leadership eventually became a part of who I am. No one is more surprised than me.

Thankfully many wonderful people walked with me during that process. Their encouragement had a refining power in my life, helping me to change the way I saw myself. Meanwhile the Lord, who is strong in our weakness, would patiently remind me that I did not choose Him, He chose me (John 15:16).

Along the way, I came to appreciate the New Testament book of First Timothy as a biblical leadership manual. In 1 Timothy 4:16, the apostle Paul specifically coached Timothy to "watch your life and doctrine closely." Why *life* as well as doctrine (ministry)? Because Paul continues, "if you do, you will save both yourself and your hearers."

Public leadership can be brutal. But it's our personal life commitments and habits that both sustain us and shape what we become. When it comes to influence, people will follow *who we are more than what we say.* To "watch your life" in this context is not selfishness or mere survival; it's the process that earns us credibility as leaders. This isn't about good looks or extroverted personalities but the content of our lives—character and conviction.

I have long believed that what we are ten years from now is largely the sum total of every today that we live. Entertainer Eddie Cantor once quipped, "It takes twenty years to make an overnight success."[1] Or, as I once heard leadership expert John Maxwell put it, "The things you do every day will eventually show." Ultimately, life is pretty daily, and that is where we start.

Several years ago, as I pondered the "watch your life" implications of 1 Timothy 4:16, I decided to write down seven phrases, two words each, that would capture the core commitments I needed to make in my own life on a daily basis. I later added to each phrase a diagnostic question to help keep my feet to the fire. (Each person can develop their own core commitments and self-test questions, but here are mine.)

> **1. KNOW GOD:** *If ministry activities were taken away from me, would I still have a growing, intimate relationship with Jesus?*

My friend Chuck Miller, in his book *The Spiritual Formation of Leaders,* describes the two rooms that every minister needs to manage—the soul room and the leadership room. He observes that "the church has tended to move type A people into leadership and the more reflective people toward prayer and spirituality. We end up forcing people to make an unnecessary choice between spirituality and leadership."[2] That's a choice we shouldn't have to make.

Do I really want my ministry to grow without my relationship with Jesus also growing? What would I want people to write on my gravestone someday: "He pastored a great church" or "He knew God"? The soul room calls us to intimacy *with* Christ apart from activity *for* Christ. This is what keeps ministry from reducing us to mere performers. Our churches are full of people who, above all, want to know that their leaders actually walk with God.

> **If we take care of the depth of our lives, God takes care of the breadth of our influence.**

Men and women who've been used by God throughout history have long known that if we take care of the depth of our lives, God takes care of the breadth of our influence. This is deep before wide, walk before work. It's pursuing brokenness more than happiness and depending on anointing more than adrenalin. It's reading and meditating on God's Word apart from the texts we are preaching on. It's seeking out fellowship with God when nobody else sees us and focusing on whatever it takes to walk in the conscious presence of God throughout the day.

No one can do this for us and no ministry success can make up for it. These are first commandment, first love issues that confront the sinister tendency within us to love leading more than we love Jesus.

> **2. PURSUE INTEGRITY:** *Are there areas of ongoing secrecy in my life that I'm intentionally hiding from those closest to me?*

Are there questionable behaviors in our lives that might trigger thoughts like *I hope my spouse never sees me doing this* or *I wouldn't want to run into anyone from church right now*? These ought to set off alarm bells inside our heads and shake us into ruthless honesty. In mathematics an integer is a whole number as opposed to a fraction. *Integrity* carries the meaning of not being fractionalized. There are no secrecy-cloaked patterns of behavior that are out of sync with our ministry roles or the God we serve.

When it comes to behaviors that compromise our integrity, the list is long—all the way from prejudice, arrogance, manipulation, lying, breaking confidences, and not keeping promises, to pornography, adulterous affairs, alcohol, illicit drugs, gambling, financial mismanagement, and embezzlement, just to name a few. Add to that demonic oppression, exhaustion, boredom, or unbridled success, and our vulnerability is only magnified.

Unfortunately, the casualties are many. The first is our own souls. It's more than a cliché to say that our secrets keep us sick. But the victims don't stop with us. The people we love and lead desperately need to be able to trust us. Where trust is violated, leadership will never work and people are always hurt. Integrity and trust are inextricably linked.

Yet in the very center of our dark, secret places God planted the cross and hung His Son on it. This is our hope—a God who meets us at our worst, calls us to the painful honesty of confession, forgives us freely, and then recreates our inner being with His resurrection Spirit. Integrity *is* possible because of this.

3. BE YOURSELF: *Am I living under the self-imposed pressure of always having to prove something to somebody?*

When we serve that relentless internal pressure to prove to others that we are good leaders or spiritual persons or able preachers, then the spotlight is still on us. We try too hard, depend on ourselves too much, and, ultimately, do foolish things. That pressure to always prove something to others about ourselves causes us to lead out of our insecurities rather than in true humility.

> At some point we need to learn from each other, but stop short of trying to be each other.

Yet the struggle to not idealize and idolize other people but to relax and be who God made us is a difficult one for most of us. The celebrity culture in the church at large doesn't help. But in the words of a rather prophetic friend of mine, "Every one of us is one of God's originals." At some point we need to learn from each other, but stop short of trying to be each other. It took me years to even come close to this place.

One of the litmus tests I have is to listen for the number of times I hear people say, "Pastor, thank you for your authenticity" or "It really helps me that you are willing to be a real person" or "I appreciate your transparency." If too many weeks go by without hearing someone say that, I know I'm slipping in the battle between image-centered professionalism and authentic, love-centered service.

When I'm winning that battle, however, I feel less pressure to perform and more freedom to just be who the Lord made me to be, without having to prove anything to anyone.

4. OWN RESPONSIBILITY: *Do I acknowledge my mistakes or do I project blame and use the pulpit to vent unresolved anger?*

Years ago, I came to the conclusion that my biggest problem in spiritual leadership is my own heart. It's not a budget shortfall or an annoying critic or a parishioner who could seriously complicate any given day in my life. Consistently, my biggest challenge is managing my heart and taking responsibility for what goes on inside of me without blaming people and circumstances for my feelings and behaviors.

When we defer responsibility for our spiritual and emotional health to others, by blaming them, we actually turn ourselves into the victims. Because we usually can't control what we blame, we end up feeling powerless and frustrated. That produces anger, which often expresses itself in destructive, self-serving leadership behaviors. People get hurt, and we stay unhealthy, as do our ministries. Only health breeds health.

Do we admit personal mistakes to our peers, or even to those we lead? Is the passion that we have when we preach the pure flow of God's Spirit, or a tainted stream of God's heart mixed with our own unresolved anger? Do we solve problems, or are we passively letting them fester? Are we always blaming our church members and our denominational leaders for everything that is wrong? Or do we own our own issues?

It takes an immense amount of spiritual courage to be truly honest with ourselves. But if we are to be people of influence, we must stop trying to control what we can't while taking responsibility for what we can—our own attitudes and behaviors.

5. EMBRACE CHANGE: *Is my attitude faith-filled and future-focused or am I overly nostalgic of the past and fearful of taking risks in the future?*

Given that change is always with us, and no growth happens without it, effective leaders choose to embrace it for what it is and determine to help others through it as well. Constantly resisting change has the reverse effect. No one grows and opportunities slip by. Nostalgia and fear take their place. Nostalgia, as wonderful as it is, can lock us into the past and make us too rigid to flex with the present. Fear, meanwhile, can paralyze us for the future. Nostalgia and fear make terrible prisons.

> **It takes immense personal courage to do what is best for the ministry as a whole, personally embracing the kinds of change that will bear fruit for Christ.**

Faith and risk-taking, on the other hand, are much more consistent with the activity of the Holy Spirit. Both require change. They demand an attitude that never settles for the predictable, the mediocre, or the safe. The test I use for monitoring the "creeping rigidity" that can immobilize in my life is whether or not I'm willing to take risks, especially as I get older. In other words, what am I planning to do next for which I am uncertain of the outcome and will need to trust God?

Unfortunately, we as ministry leaders often expect everyone to change except us. A pastor of a revitalized church once told me that what amazed him most about the church's turnaround was the degree to which he as the pastor had to change before anything else changed. It's easy to fall into the trap of expecting more of others than we do of ourselves. When we refuse to change, we will lead only in ways that meet our needs and conform to our familiar routines and blind spots. But it takes immense personal courage to do what is best for the ministry as a whole, personally embracing the kinds of change that will bear fruit for Christ.

For most of us constructive, personal change requires that others walk with us, speak into our lives, hold us to our priorities, and constantly keep the big ministry perspective in front of us. It's a hard journey to take alone.

6. LOVE LEARNING: *Am I coasting intellectually, or am I applying myself to the disciplines of personal study and reflection?*

When he was languishing in prison, Paul asked for his books (2 Tim. 4:13). We easily forget that Paul was a ministry leader, yes, but a scholar as well. He was extremely well educated for his day and, judging by the way that he thought and wrote, likely had a genius level IQ. Unfortunately, our church experiences have sometimes communicated the subtle but erroneous impression that a person cannot be spiritual and smart at the same time.

The Scriptures, however, call us to the *renewing* of our minds, not the neglect of our minds. I will never forget hearing one of my spiritual leaders say, "I want to live 'til I die." We probably all know people who have stopped living a long time before they actually died simply because they stopped being curious about people, about the world the Lord has created, and about the great theological truths He has revealed.

By the time I reached my mid-forties, it was surprising to me how strong the temptation had become simply to coast the second half of my ministry life. It's distressingly easy to let up on personal and intellectual disciplines, replacing them with too much television, social media, preoccupation with sports, and low-effort activities that waste time and require nothing of us. But we can do better than preparing messages with minimal study and wasting our minds on idle things.

We can read books, connect with people who have accomplished more than we have, ask questions, always listen, write down ideas, keep files, learn from life experiences—these are some of the more productive and fulfilling ways we can live and continually grow as leaders. A lot of the reading and learning I do are related to my leadership responsibilities, but it's especially fun when it doesn't stop there. On vacations I like to read physics books as well as biographies of American presidents. Keeping up with the news and current events is also a fairly daily activity most of the year.

While we need to rely entirely on the Holy Spirit, there is no excuse for shallowness on our part. Jesus told us to love the Lord our God with, among other things, "all your mind" (Matt. 22:37).

7. LIVE JOYFULLY: *Do I love what I'm doing or have I taken the pressures of ministry onto myself?*

While I was studying engineering at the University of Minnesota, I was also leading an Assemblies of God campus group (Chi Alpha) that had shrunk from twelve people down to three by the end of my senior year. But during my second year of graduate school the Lord gave us a supernatural breakthrough, and we grew overnight to over sixty students, then a hundred.

Unfortunately, still being a novice leader and a full-time student, my insecurities got the best of me. I began to feel immense pressure for everything that went on. If anything went wrong, I took it as evidence that I wasn't a good leader. Yet the group was growing and the imperfections were multiplying.

Late one night, as I was worrying and beating myself up again, I sensed the Holy Spirit direct me to start praying differently whenever a problem in the ministry came up. Some of my friends call it the "Bradford prayer," and it goes like this: "Lord, You have another problem in Your ministry. So what are You going to do about it? And, by the way, if You need any help, I'm available."

In other words, God was helping me to off-load the pressure from myself onto Him. Trite formulas usually aren't much help to me, but this simple prayer is potent. The ministries God calls us to aren't ours—they belong to Him, and He can carry them. We take responsibility to watch our hearts and steward His calling on our lives, but He carries the weight. He bears the yoke with us and makes it light (Matt. 11:28–30).

Our ministries may not be perfect, but we can still serve with joy because the pressure is on Him, not us.

No matter what they are, the core personal commitments we make define the things that will shape who we become and how we lead. Let's take care of our own hearts before we try to fix the hearts of others. Who we are will take us further than what we do.

CHAPTER 2

A Spiritual Center

*"Your name and renown
are the desire of our hearts."*
ISAIAH 26:8

People who watch us lead often assume that it's easy for us to stay spiritually strong in the ministry. Sometimes, as a pastor, people would say to me, "I wish I had a job like yours. It would be great to just pray and read God's Word all the time." That, of course, is not reality. Ministry leadership can actually be quite toxic to spiritual health. We often pray too little and work too hard. Our identities get more wrapped up in our busyness than in our life with God. We can actually slip into loving leadership more than we love Jesus.

In his book, *The Life and Teaching of Jesus Christ*, Scottish preacher James Steward surveyed the landscape of religious leadership in Jesus' time and noted that...

The Pharisees had *externalized* religion.
The scribes had *professionalized* religion.
The Sadducees had *secularized* religion.
The Zealots had *nationalized* religion.[3]

If we're not careful, that is exactly what public ministry could do to us as well—externalize us, professionalize us, disillusion us, and make us far too political.

Or, as Eugene Peterson put it in *The Jesus Way*,

> Religion is one of the best covers for sin of almost all kinds. Pride, anger, lust, and greed are vermin that flourish under the floorboards of religion. Those of us who are identified with institutions or vocations in religion can't be too vigilant. The devil does some of his best work behind stained glass.[4]

Tim Elmore attaches some helpful profiles to these spiritual dangers. Have we, perhaps, fallen victim to one or more of these ministry-active counterfeits ourselves?

> *THE STARVING BAKER*—We are too busy providing bread for others to eat. The short-term result is that we feed others while starving ourselves.
> *THE SUPERFICIAL CELEBRITY*—We keep others at a distance, including God, as we try to guard ourselves from being hurt or manipulated or being discovered as an imperfect leader.
> *THE POLISHED PERFORMER*—We are overly concerned with the "show" we do. If we perform long enough, we may find it hard to ever be genuine with God again.
> *THE SPIRITUAL PROFESSIONAL*—We perceive spirituality as our job, a 9 a.m. to 5 p.m. deal, or an "every Sunday" event where we try to turn on our relationship with God on demand.[5]

Over my years of pastoral ministry, I've found that the best antidote to the toxic tendencies of ministry leadership is to live within the life-giving constraints of three biblical experiences: (1) being broken before God, (2) abiding with Christ in His Word and prayer, and (3) living in the fellowship of the Holy Spirit.

Broken Before God

Understandably, the notion of brokenness grates against most every human instinct we have. Yet spiritual disciplines

A SPIRITUAL CENTER

alone, apart from the experience of being brought to the end of ourselves, can still leave us shallow. "A broken and contrite heart" (Ps. 51:17) is still the doorway to spiritual intimacy with Christ. Our self-driven tendencies will resist this and or our preference for the security of rigid disciplines will seek to replace this, but nothing can substitute for a true brokenness before the Lord.

I've always been moved by how eyewitness Frank Bartleman described the famous Azusa Street Revival:

> In that old building, with its low rafters and bare floors, God took strong men and women to pieces, and put them together again, for His glory. It was a tremendous overhauling process: Pride and self-assertion, self-importance and self-esteem, could not survive there.[6]

God forbid that we ever become impressed with ourselves. May He, indeed, take us to pieces and put us together again for His glory. Or, in the incisive words of A. W, Tozer, "It is doubtful whether God can bless a man greatly until He has hurt him deeply."

> **God's hand is both gracious and sufficiently severe enough to break all that resists or replaces Him.**

Jesus warned us, "Apart from me you can do nothing" (John 15:5). What worries me most about that statement is the period at the end. He does not say, "Apart from me you can do nothing ... unless you find the right worship leader or until you finish your degree." It's a humbling and unqualified assertion: "Apart from me you can do nothing." This realization is where brokenness takes us.

When Jesus took the five loaves and two fish, He blessed them and then He broke them. In doing so, the food multiplied miraculously. In much the same way, God-dependence is forged in us. We are blessed with calling, anointing, and favor—but we, too, need to be broken if we are to be multiplied. Self-dependence, self-will, and self-interest all die hard. Yet God's hand is both gracious and sufficiently severe enough to break all that resists or replaces Him.

Miles Sanford would often exhort believers, "Abide above—for your life below." In his book, *Principles of Spiritual Growth*,[7] he lists the names of great heroes of the faith from the past couple of centuries—people like Jonathan Goforth, D. L. Moody, Amy Carmichael, John Hyde, Hudson Taylor, George Mueller, and many others. He then makes the striking observation that, on average, it took fifteen years for these extremely fruitful spiritual leaders to go from "working for Christ" to "Christ working through them." That is what the Lord is after when He breaks us.

God gave me a small but potent taste of this when I transferred to the University of Minnesota for my junior year as an engineering student. It would turn out to be the most spiritually disillusioning year of my life. I became involved with a small campus ministry group that had started at the university a few years earlier, but all of the leaders were transitioning out. Towards the end of that year, the campus pastor, Reverend K. K. John, asked me to take over and make it a purely student-led group. I reluctantly said yes. A year later there were only three of us left. My calling into engineering seemed to be confirmed.

One day, one of the other two guys still coming to the group, Steve, was visiting me in my dorm room. A moment came when he simply said, "Maybe we should fast and pray." Surprisingly and suddenly, the Spirit of God gripped my heart. I became desperately hungry for God. Sometimes it even took away my hunger for food for days. Between classes or late at nights, for weeks on end, I was driven to pray. And it was messy praying. Sometimes all I could do was lie on my face on the floor and groan.

Although the intensity of that experience lifted somewhat after a few months, nothing dramatic happened for the next year and a half except that our group grew back to about a dozen. Mainly, people joined us who felt an urgency to pray for the campus. Then the breakthrough came, overnight and without warning.

On a normal Tuesday evening, midway through the fall semester of my second year of graduate school, when I fully expected to see the normal twelve in attendance, over sixty students suddenly showed up. They came in individual clusters of friends but all on the same night. To this day I have no human explanation for how that could have happened. But even more importantly, the Spirit of God came powerfully upon us that evening and nothing was ever the same again.

> We must recover a basic dependence on God, no matter what it takes. Brokenness is the pathway.

Soon the group grew to nearly a hundred, eventually becoming a university church. I can trace my own journey into full-time ministry when I finished my graduate degree three and a half years later back to the breakthrough God gave us that day. But I will always remember that the seeds of that breakthrough were planted when I was at my lowest, when my first attempts at leadership had failed. Although every one of our specific stories as ministry leaders will be different, the need is the same. We must recover a basic dependence on God, no matter what it takes. Brokenness is the pathway. Without it our ministries will amount to little more than what we can accomplish on our own.

Abiding in the Word and Prayer

After establishing that nothing of eternal significance can be accomplished without Him (John 15:5), Jesus then paints a word picture inviting us to Himself. A branch needs to stay attached to a vine for life to flow into it. So, "If you remain in me and my words remain in you, ask whatever you wish, and it will be done for you" (John 15:7). Both the King James and the English Standard versions seize on the relationally-textured verb "abide" in order to translate the verb in the critical conditional clause—"If you abide in me..."

Experiences of brokenness come to us in seasons, but to "remain," to "abide," to stay connected to Jesus' life is a vitality-charged relationship that transcends seasons and shapes the spiritual center of our lives. And it's a two-way street. His words abide in us, and we abide in him. This is an invitation to engage the Scriptures and embrace a life of prayer.

Engaging Scripture

"Take the helmet of salvation and the sword of the Spirit which is the word of God" (Eph. 6:17).

Just as I had finished my degrees in engineering and was transitioning into full-time ministry at the University of Minnesota, I encountered a children's evangelist who had impacted my life quite powerfully as a child. After getting reacquainted, he proceeded to show me his "speed reading" Bible. Each page had just one column down the center, with a wide margin on each side. Somehow I had grown up with the impression that when it comes to reading God's Word, slowly is holy. But here was a man of God who had taught himself to speed read, and now digested close to forty chapters of Scripture a day.

Then he said, "I haven't changed anything in my ministry with kids. I use the same puppets, the same chalk drawings, and the same children's songs. But since I've begun absorbing Scripture like this on a daily basis, God's Spirit has been moving in my services in ways that I've never experienced before." I'll never forget the impact that made on me. The Word and the Spirit work together. The Word is the *sword* the Spirit uses (Eph. 6:17). If Jesus' Word abides in us, then we'll walk in truth and God's Spirit will be active, nourishing us with spiritual vitality.

Let me suggest three ways of engaging Scriptures:

> **Reading**—Hopefully the demands of ministry leadership will never eclipse our hunger to simply read God's Word on a continual basis. It may not be forty chapters a day, but most of us will need a plan to stay on course. I personally

try to sit down three or four times a week and, each time, sequentially read two chapters of Old Testament history, two full pages of the Psalms, one chapter of Proverbs (corresponding to the date of the month—like Proverbs 26 on the twenty-sixth), one chapter from the Gospels, one chapter from Acts, and two chapters from the New Testament letters and Revelation. On Sundays I break up the routine and focus on a list of life verses and favorite Scriptures that I have bookmarked in the Bible app on my phone.

Meditating—As I read these chapters, I look for one verse to return to at the end and meditate on. It will either be a verse that leaps out of the page at me, or one that at least catches my attention in some way. Biblical meditation has the idea of repetition at its heart, along with time and thoughtfulness. I usually take about five minutes to mediate on that one verse, reading it over a number of times and asking the Lord to speak to me through it. Taking time to meditate on Scripture is one way to develop an ear for the voice of the Holy Spirit as God speaks to us through His Word.

Listening—Because the Spirit and the Word work together, God will often use Scripture to speak to us, whether it be a promise or a prompting to act or a passage that may become a "life Scripture." While I always try to be attentive to the context and the author's intent, I also don't want to miss God's voice as He brings particular Scriptures alive to me personally. I don't want to simply read God's Word; I want God's Word to read me in all of its challenging, encouraging dimensions.

Embracing Prayer

"When you pray, go into your room, close the door and pray to your Father, who is unseen. Then your Father, who sees what is done in secret, will reward you"(Matt. 6:6).

> **I believe that seeking God in private is what puts the fragrance of His favor and anointing upon our public ministries.**

I'm a strong proponent of corporate, agreeing prayer. When mountains need moving and spiritual warfare is intense, it helps immensely to find others to pray with. But in Matthew 6:6 Jesus also taught us to seek God alone, behind closed doors. He, in fact, attached reward to it. Praying with others may move mountains, but I believe that seeking God in private is what puts the fragrance of His favor and anointing upon our public ministries.

Although we often experience debilitating guilt over our personal prayer lives, we must not give up or let it shut us down. Here are a few suggestions for growing our prayerfulness.

> **Pray with Yieldedness**—Make time spent in prayer more than just working through a long prayer list, as commendable as that may be. Praying, above all, should be an encounter with the presence of Jesus. Take time to worship, pray in tongues, repent, and hunger for the Holy Spirit. Yield to Jesus' presence and let prayer become a relationship of intimacy and mutuality with God. Make it more than a duty or a chore. Ask God to help you to make Him your chief desire and greatest delight.
>
> **Pray the Scriptures**—This became an important spiritual discipline of mine as a pastoral leader. When my mind would wander, praying back to God the text of Scripture helped me to focus my heart. When I was hurting, passages of Scripture like Psalms 30–33 would put language both to my pain and to my need. When it was hard to know how to pray, letting the content of Scripture shape the subject of my prayer helped me to know that I was praying God's will. Praying Scripture took the pressure off and drew me into the Spirit's presence.

A SPIRITUAL CENTER

Pray in Faith—Prayer can easily become more of an exercise in worry than an exercise in faith. When we pray and intercede, we focus on many difficult issues. Sometimes I felt fine when I started to pray but felt burdened down by the end of my prayer time. Still, faith reframes everything. It thrives on praise, thanksgiving, and confidence in God's promises. Faith sees past circumstances and believes for breakthroughs. It possesses answers from God in the invisible realm so they will be released in the visible realm. Praying with faith changes the whole posture of prayer. With it, we please God (Heb. 11:6).

Living in the Fellowship of the Holy Spirit

"May the grace of the Lord Jesus Christ, and the love of God, and the fellowship of the Holy Spirit be with you all" (2 Cor. 13:14).

Because it's easy to reduce our spiritual lives to a set of do's, don'ts, and disciplines, we often miss the heart of what it is to be a Christian: having a personal, intimate relationship with Jesus. I often tell people, "Before trying to spend an hour a day with God, try spending twenty-four hours a day with God." This is a lifestyle of fellowship with the Holy Spirit all day long, walking with Him, talking to Him, listening to Him, and living in His conscious presence.

Two things help me with this: (1) intentionally staying grateful and (2) praying in the Spirit. Paul coaches us to pray with thankfulness (Phil. 4:6). This keeps us aware of God's activity behind every good thing in our lives (James 1:17). In 1 Corinthians 14:14 Paul also reminds us that when we pray in tongues, the Holy Spirit prays through us. So praising God and praying in the Spirit help me to walk in fellowship with the Holy Spirit no matter where I am or what I'm doing throughout the day. Ministry leadership doesn't have to be toxic to our spiritual health. We can walk in fellowship with the Holy Spirit, abide in Christ, and find God's grace strong in our weakness.

CHAPTER 3

A Serving Identity

"For who is greater, the one who is at the table or the one who serves?
Is it not the one who is at the table?
But I am among you as one who serves."
    Luke 22:27

The "me-first" problem is as old as the human heart. When confronted with the choice between God's way and their way, Adam and Eve chose their way. After finally preaching in Ninevah, Jonah got angry that God had mercy on the city. His own prejudices crowded out God's heart.

And on a road trip to Capernaum, Jesus' disciples hung back, hopefully out of earshot, arguing over who was greatest. Like boys with beards, they were still trying to resolve their identity issues, fighting over who was where in the pecking order. Then, in Matthew 20, Mama Zebedee entered the fray, reminding Jesus that in His kingdom He will only have two sides—His right hand and His left. Unfortunately, He had twelve disciples. Her solution? "My two boys" of course.

The me-first problem infects ministry leaders today as well. Unless marched to the cross and crucified, the preoccupation with ourselves will eventually undermine our leadership. Yet we build a set of misbeliefs around it:

"As a leader I'm entitled to special privileges."
"Anything I do in leadership must ultimately benefit me."
"My team is here to make me look good."
"I should be paid what I'm worth."
"People who disagree with me are my enemies."
"I'll neglect others to protect myself"
"Controlling people is how I get my way"

This issue of control is the one that Jesus picked up on at the end of His conversation with Peter and John's mother: "Jesus called them together and said, 'You know that the rulers of the Gentiles lord it over them, and their high officials exercise authority over them. Not so with you'" (Matt. 20:25–26).

Although effective leaders need to be decisive and directional, Jesus' words, *"Not so with you,"* clearly put boundaries around how we are to motivate and treat people in the process. Rather than dominating and controlling, Jesus calls us to a higher way: leading like servants.

Three Kinds of Power

As leaders, any move towards servant-likeness and away from me-centeredness ultimately brings us face to face with the issue of *power* and how we use it in our lives. Power in human relationships has to do with the influence we have and how we exert it. There are essentially three kinds of relational power:[8]

> **Positional Power**—We have this power by virtue of the title on our office doors and the authority that our roles or positions give us. Parents, for instance, understand positional power. When all else fails it comes down to, "I am the parent and you are not, so do what I say."
>
> **Possessional Power**—We have this power because of something we have that others do not. Some countries have weapons that others do not have; some church members have more money than other church members; some ministry partners have more education or more knowledge

about a particular situation than others. The possession of whatever that thing may be is what gives leverage and influence to that person in relationship to others.

Personal Power—This power flows out of the trust and respect others have for us. It is influence that is rooted in who we are, based on inner character and proven integrity rather than external position or personal possessions. Even though he may never preach again to crowded stadiums, Billy Graham exemplifies well this kind of power—the influential power of an admired, respected life.

Our insecurities and the prideful, darker sides of our egos tend to drive us to operate out of positional power. But Jesus tries to push us to operate out of personal power. The Gentiles (Romans), in all of their positional power (governing authority) and their possessional power (weapons), *"lord it over you,"* Jesus said. But we are not to be like them.

Instead, Jesus calls us to think and act like servants, not masters. This radically changes the way we view ourselves as leaders. We are facilitators, not superstars; coaches, not dictators; shepherds, not professionals. Our focus is on bringing out the best in others rather than serving ourselves. The ministries we lead this

> **Our focus is on bringing out the best in others rather than serving ourselves.**

way become less personality-driven and more people-centered. We are passionate about *everyone* being used by God, not just us. Servant leaders lift up the people around them and cheer them on.

Ironically, this is precisely what gives Christ-like leaders immense influence. People want to follow leaders who love them, believe in them, and help them reach their potential. Usually, the people I have influenced the most don't necessarily remember any particular sermon I preached, but they do remember the time I took to be with them and to encourage them.

A central axiom of leadership is that people will tend to rise to what we expect of them. If we value and trust people, they'll want to step up to the potential they believe we see in them. And if they also witness in our personal lives qualities they admire and respect, they'll be drawn to following our example. This is leading out of personal power.

But when we manipulate and control people, the opposite happens. People either resist us or they comply externally but don't commit internally. Highly controlling leaders may, indeed, get people doing what they want them to do, but rarely do they bring out the best in others. Dominating people and bossing them around only leaves them resentful and angry. Healthy people will not put up with it, and leadership-gifted people will stay away from us.

Our insecurities, of course, aggravate the problem. They will either make us too *self-promoting* or too *self-protecting*. If we come across as self-promoting, people will feel like we are using them to advance our egos and agendas. If we behave in self-protecting ways, teams will find it frustrating to work with us because we'll make leadership decisions based on our needs rather than what is best for the ministry. It's far too easy to put off dealing with hard issues in order to protect ourselves from emotional anxiety or relational tension or anything that might threaten our public image.

Servant leadership, on the other hand, puts the mission to serve Christ and those He places around us ahead of our me-first tendencies. It's also perfectly consistent with a Christ-centered, Spirit-empowered spirituality. Godly spirituality in leadership is best expressed when we serve others. I like to think of it as being "reduced to greatness." Christ-likeness will always make servants out of us. Serving, in turn, will transform us into leaders who empower others—exactly the kind of leaders they want to follow. This Jesus calls "greatness."

In the next two verses of Matthew 20, after declaring, *"Not so with you"* when it comes to *"lording it over"* people, Jesus described what this "reducing" journey would look like (vv. 27–28). Along the way we will encounter both a *renunciation* and a *resolution*.

A SERVING IDENTITY

When Jesus Reduces Us to Greatness . . .

"Not so with you. Instead, whoever wants to become great among you must be your servant, and whoever wants to be first must be your slave"(Matt. 20:26–27).

> . . . *we renounce the myth that the world owes us something.*

The biggest problem with believing the world owes us something is that we're probably the only ones in our world who actually believe that. Most people aren't sitting around thinking about what they owe us. Buying into that myth, in fact, only sets us up for a lot of disappointment in life. It is me-first at its worst.

Servants don't think or act like consumers. I once heard Hal Donaldson, executive director of Convoy of Hope, remind a room full of spiritual leaders that we're in trouble when we find ourselves spending more time asking ourselves, "Who is serving me?" than "Who am I serving?" There's a world of difference between those two questions. Servants can't afford to be preoccupied with what others are or are not doing for them. Neither do they worry about the spotlight being on them.

In a church I pastored a number of years ago, we put on our annual Sunday evening Christmas program. Everyone was involved from children to adults, actors to singers, stagehands to pastors. At the end of the program we gave out gifts of appreciation and expressed thanks to everyone who participated. I couldn't help but notice, however, that I was the only one who was left out.

As ashamed as I am to admit it, I went home angry, thinking to myself, *No one has any idea of the work I invested behind the scenes to make this evening happen.* As the pastor, I was also the public host for the event and the one who brought the evangelistic message at the end. But when the recognitions were passed out, I was the only person not mentioned, and it really bothered me.

Self-pity is like quicksand, and the Lord had to deal strongly with my heart to get me out of it. At one point I sensed the Spirit of God say to me, "Jim, you have to stop counting the thank-you notes. I thought you were doing this for Me, not for the appreciation."

As hard as it was to feel unappreciated, that experience helped me get back in touch with my own version of being a servant to all. I had to renounce again the myth that anybody owed me anything, including appreciation, so I could reaffirm that Jesus and His glory are the real and only reasons that I serve.

> *. . . we resolve to put more into life than we hope to take out of it.*

In the next verse, Jesus brings us to a resolution; He reduces us to greatness: *". . . just as the Son of Man did not come to be served, but to serve, and to give his life as a ransom for many"* (Matt. 20:28).

When I was in my twenties, just learning about leadership, I had the opportunity to read J. Oswald Sander's classic, *Spiritual Leadership.* In it he described an important trait of a spiritual leader—"He aims to put more into life than he takes out of it."[9] It made an indelible impression on me. What if I actually made the decision to live that way—ahead of time, up front and early in my life? Or what if I insisted, instead, that everything I invested into life and ministry through the years was conditioned on it benefiting me back at least as much, or more?

Sanders brought me face to face with the realization that leadership is about influence, not fairness. This is how Jesus lived. He didn't come to even the score or insist on reciprocity but to give His life. This is counter-intuitive for us. When we buy things or transact business, we want the reassurance that if we put money out we will get something of equal or greater value back. Jesus steers us differently.

I like to think of people as being either "thermostats" or "thermometers." Thermostats reflect the surrounding temperature, but thermostats set it. Leaders need to be like thermostats: influencing their surroundings rather than yielding to them. They don't wait around for someone else to step out before them or instead of them. They understand that changing the world will probably require them to make investments in others with no guarantee of return.

A SERVING IDENTITY

Wycliffe missionary Bernie May, in his book *Learning to Trust*,[10] describes an encounter with the Mazatec Indians in southwestern Mexico. Although wonderful people, there was a cultural peculiarity to them that was rooted in a concept of "limited good." If asked, "Who taught you to bake bread?" the answer would be "I just know." They would seldom wish each other well and were hesitant to teach each other. Their belief was that there was only so much "good" to go around. To wish others well would irretrievably diminish their own wellbeing; to teach another would mean less knowledge for themselves; to love a second child would mean having to love the first child less. This is a scarcity mentality—the belief that life is a pie, and there are only so many pieces to go around.

> **Leaders who change the world decide, up front, to put more into life than they ever hope to take out of it.**

In the kingdom of God, there is no "limited good," only abundance. Leaders who change the world decide, up front, to put more into life than they ever hope to take out of it. It is a life-resolve that makes them risk-takers and mentors. They never read a book just for themselves; they read it with an eye to who else it might benefit. They network people together, even if they aren't at the center, and they encourage potential in others even if it eclipses their own.

They come at life and leadership the way Jesus did. He came not to be served, but to give His life away. And amazingly, like Jesus, our lives are not diminished when we live like that. They are, in fact, multiplied. This is abundant living. It breaks us out of the limitations of me-first preoccupations and turns us into thermostats, people of influence for God's glory.

The Foundation of Humility

The renunciation of self-interest and the resolve to put more into life than we expect back are both founded on humility.

There is no serving of others without it. Unfortunately, humility and meekness are terribly underrated, especially when it comes to leading. Yet they are both extremely potent and influential! Humility attracts the grace of God and aligns us with His favor: "God opposes the proud but shows favor to the humble" (James 4:6).

Meekness is not insecurity. Truly meek people are strong because they are confident in both their identity and their destiny. *"Blessed are the meek, for they will inherit the earth" (Matt. 5:5).*

Humility and meekness are also incredibly freeing. They don't make us weak or indecisive as leaders. They have nothing to do with timidity or shyness. Instead, they unlock our potential to serve by releasing us from slavery to things that could limit our leadership potential and even shut us down. After all, humility and meekness free us from the need to . . .

- prove anything to anyone
- impress others or promote ourselves
- feel superior to others in order to feel good about ourselves
- always have the last word
- always defend ourselves to every critic
- hold on to our rights at the cost of depriving others
- be appreciated or paid adequately for our leadership
- control other people's feelings and behaviors in order to get our way

Meekness releases our hearts to lovingly care for people without dominating them. Humility puts our confidence and our welfare into the hands of God and frees us to reach out to people in spite of the risks. Taken together, humility and meekness relocate our identities away from the shaky foundations of our self-doubts and imbed them in the timeless love and calling of God, making us bold and courageous.

This brings us back to the core of our spirituality. The pathway to meekness is not beating ourselves down, but abiding in Jesus and becoming more like the servant He is. In the poignantly perceptive words of Phillip Brooks:

> "The true way to be humble is not to stoop until you are smaller than yourself, but to stand at your real height against some higher nature that will show you what the real smallness of your greatness is."[11]

That higher nature is Jesus, and He is constantly reducing us to greatness. We stand up to His measure, not our own. And while our fallen human natures are bent on seeking position and popularity, Jesus went the other way:

> *Because we the children of Adam*
> *want to become great,*
> *He became small;*
> *Because we will not stoop,*
> *He humbled Himself;*
> *Because we want to rule,*
> *He came to serve.*[12]
> *[unknown]*

SECTION 2

Systems and Strategies

The subways ("tubes") in London have a recorded message that plays every time the doors open: "Mind the gap." It's the British way of saying 'Don't trip over the space between the subway floor and the station floor."

There's another kind of "gap" in life that needs minding as well—the gap between what we expect and what we experience; that disconnect between ideal and real. The gap between what we hope for and what we end up with gets especially wide in ministry, and it's easy to trip over. It can leave us disappointed with ourselves and feeling little more than helpless victims of choices people make or circumstances over which we have no control. If not minded properly, that gap can exhaust us, wearing us down with frustration and even anger. It's certainly the stuff that discouragement is made of.

One way to cope with the gap is to project blame on others, rationalize away our personal responsibility and cave into cynicism. The other, equally unhelpful, way is to simply toss out our expectations and give up completely on the hope of a better future. Either way will paralyze us.

Godly leaders fill that gap with both faith and a God-given plan. Faith is a gift of God's Spirit as well as a personal choice to trust His character, no matter what we see. It's rooted deep in our spirituality. A God-given plan is what keeps us moving forward, focused on the things that we can do, not the things we can't control.

Just as we have faith to see Christ's church grow, King David had faith to see God's temple built. But he also had specific Spirit-inspired plans that he passed on to Solomon: "He [David] gave him [Solomon] the plans of all that the Spirit had put in his mind for the courts of the temple of the Lord" (1 Chron. 28:12).

These plans involved God-given systems, structural outlines, and coordinated work assignments. Eventually, what David envisioned was realized by his son with the completion of the temple, and the gap was gone. As ministry leaders, the Holy Spirit can also give us plans for organizational systems and strategies that will work in parallel with our faith, until vision becomes reality. These plans we will explore now.

CHAPTER 4

Oversight Roles

*"All this," David said, "I have in writing as a result of the LORD's hand on me,
and he enabled me to understand all the details of the plan."*
1 CHRONICLES 28:19

Leadership is more than surviving next Sunday or making it through another board meeting or responding to yet another crisis. Leadership sees the big picture. Leadership peers into the future and points the direction to go. Leadership lifts people up and helps them to achieve their God-given potential. Leadership encourages people to work together in teams, and leadership gets out of the way to help others use their ministry gifts. Leadership clings to faith when others get nervous.

But how does leadership like that work? What are the most important things for ministry leaders to focus on in order to move people forward into God's purposes for them?

In Luke 6:12–19 we meet Jesus the leader. Here, in three sequential events at a pivotal moment in His earthly ministry, Jesus timelessly modeled three primary characteristics of ministry leadership: it is *spiritual, relational,* and *missional.* These become the starting points for understanding our own oversight roles as ministry leaders.

Ministry Leadership Is Spiritual

"Jesus went out to a mountainside to pray, and spent the night praying to God" (Luke 6:12).

First and foremost, Jesus always integrated spiritual dynamics into his leadership—forty days of fasting before His ministry, nights of prayer during His ministry, and a lifestyle of unbroken communion with the Father throughout His ministry. Here in Luke 6:12 Jesus prayed all night before making an important leadership move.

Overseeing and cultivating spiritual vitality is a central responsibility of ministry leaders. For the early church this meant the upper room before the outer courts, the day of Pentecost before world-changing ministry, and an unrelenting lifestyle of seeking God no matter what else they did. Our lives personally need a healthy spiritual center, but so do the ministries we lead. We're dependent entirely on the Holy Spirit working with us. Ministry leadership is a partnership with God.

At a particularly plateaued time in my own pastoral ministry, the Lord spoke to me to go into the church sanctuary several days a week, walk the rows of seats, and do nothing but pray in the Spirit for an hour. The church was doing fine, but I had come to the end of my creativity and had run out of ideas. Although I was maintaining fairly well, I was at a loss as to how to lead the church to the next level.

By obediently walking that sanctuary and praying in tongues, the Lord made it possible for me to meet Him at the end of myself. He offloaded the pressure of the church's future from me and took it onto Himself. The Holy Spirit prayed through me the mind of the Father (Rom. 8:27) when my mind had no idea what to pray anymore. In the years that followed, I found a certain effortlessness in leading the church that I hadn't experienced earlier.

Jesus-styled leadership is first of all spiritual. It is praying hard, having faith, and staying full of the Holy Spirit. It is seeing people encounter God and watching His Spirit do things we can't humanly account for.

OVERSIGHT ROLES

Ministry Leadership Is Relational

"When morning came, he called his disciples to him and chose twelve of them, whom he also designated apostles" (Luke 6:13).

Jesus knew that preaching to large crowds alone wouldn't serve His greater mission. In his classic book, *The Master Plan of Evangelism,* Robert Coleman writes: "While the church is looking for methods to move the multitudes, God is looking for men [and women] whom the multitudes will follow."[13] People are God's agenda. So immediately after spending all night in prayer, Jesus chose twelve men to be with Him and to share His authority.

I have often heard a significant mentor in my life, Dr. George Wood, say "ministry flows out of relationship." The kingdom of God is relational to its core. Jesus understood that and lived it. At some point early in our leadership lives we, too, need to take responsibility for having people around us who know us well, know how to pray for us specifically, and know how to partner with us in ministry. We dare not lead alone.

> **Jesus made the decision to not only minister to people but through people.**

Except for praying, getting the right people around us doing the right things is some of the hardest and most important work we do as leaders. If we're intimidated by having strong people on our team, we'll hold onto ministry too tightly and become far too controlling. This will devalue and demotivate gifted people around us, eventually pushing them away from us. As one pastor friend of mine put it, "We take the smartest people in our churches and put them in the most mindless roles."

In spite of our insecurities, there's a better way to lead, and Jesus modeled it. Early in His ministry He decided to balance the demands of ministering to the multitudes with the time it took to invest in a small circle of twelve potential leaders. The ministry-empowering fire of the Holy Spirit would later fall on them at Pentecost, and Jesus' church would begin to grow.

In essence, Jesus made the decision to not only minister to people but through people. To this day, the growth of many ministries is dependent on that pivotal leadership decision. For Jesus, this meant intentional relationship with His disciples in all of its dimensions—fellowship, training, and accountability. Today we would call this nurturing and networking. As ministry leaders, one of our key oversight responsibilities is to nurture relationships with those we lead and facilitate networks of relationships between those we lead.

Ministry Leadership Is Missional

Immediately after praying through the night and then choosing His closest associates, Jesus "went down with them" into a large crowd, according to Luke 6:17. "Those troubled by impure spirits were cured, and the people all tried to touch him, because power was coming from him and healing them all" (Luke 6:17–19). Leadership that is spiritual and relational must also become leadership that is missional. Inwardness and lack of vision to reach lost people misses the heart of God and is fatal to our future.

In Acts 1:8, Jesus clearly linked Spirit and mission: "But you will receive power when the Holy Spirit comes on you; and you will be my witnesses in Jerusalem, and in all Judea and Samaria, and to the ends of the earth." We can't be Pentecostal in identity if we aren't missional in priority and activity. The baptism of the Holy Spirit does more than make us feel better. It sends us into the world and equips us with the power we need to reach people for Christ.

The great missionary-minded pastor from Canada, Oswald J. Smith, wrote in his convicting book, *The Cry of the World*, "We should have kept before us our Lord's post-resurrection commands. We should have evangelized the world. Otherwise we have no ground for our existence as a church. There is no reason why we should have churches unless they are reaching out to those who have never heard."[14]

Every ministry needs a mission. Effective ministry leaders

never lose sight of that and never stop working towards it. They feel the responsibility to do whatever it takes to remove obstacles to reaching lost and hurting people. Missional leaders unapologetically seek results, solve problems, and find ways to get things done, never taking refuge in the predictable or the familiar or the safe. Jesus said "Go," so they refuse to sit.

Ministry Leadership Is Also Organizational

So far we've seen that Jesus modeled ministry leadership that was spiritual, relational, and missional, thus providing a strategic template for our own oversight priorities as ministry leaders. But it is *organizational structure* that functionally connects the spiritual, relational, and missional together. It constitutes the fourth focus of a leader.

One of my favorite leadership verses is ...

The horse is made ready for the day of battle, but victory rests with the Lord. Proverbs 21:31

Here we have pictured a holistic partnership between God's Spirit and our stewardship. The emphasis is on the right thing. There is no victory without the Lord. But making ready the "horse" for battle is our part. Good administrative systems won't usher in revival or bring spiritual breakthroughs, but without some kind of structural order, sustainable ministry that conserves the fruit of renewal won't be possible.

A successful young entrepreneur who served on one of my church boards once explained to me, "I'm not necessarily smarter than other people, just better organized." While many of our personal strengths as ministry leaders may lean toward relationship building and pastoral care, the basic organizational skills needed for leadership can still be learned in a way that stays true to our personalities and God's anointing on our lives. The key is *intentionality*. There's a profound difference between *leading* and simply *responding*. Being intentional is what makes the difference.

Flexing for emergencies and fighting off distractions is an inevitable part of any leader's life. But good leadership is more than just being dragged from crisis to crisis all the time. It's deciding up front the most important things that we should be doing and then determining to not sacrifice those priorities to matters of secondary importance. Getting out of reactionary mode and having a system, or strategy, for staying focused on our key leadership roles is what makes the difference.

The first of the Four Spiritual Laws[15] developed by Dr. Bill Bright, is a famous one: "God loves you and offers a wonderful

> **Good leadership requires scheduling our priorities into our calendars before other people fill our calendars for us.**

plan for your life." Unfortunately, I discovered as a pastor that there were a lot of people in my life who also loved me and had a wonderful plan for my life. Good leadership requires scheduling our priorities into our calendars before other people fill our calendars for us. That is intentionality.

Here is how it all fits together.

S-M-O-R: Spirit, Mission, Organization, and Relationship

Many of us have experienced the delight of sitting around a camp fire while someone pulls out the graham crackers, chocolate bars, and marshmallows. Everyone knows what that means: s'mores! In an effort to keep things simple and hopefully memorable, let me take the four core components of ministry leadership that we've been exploring (spirit, relationship, mission, and organization) and rearrange them into my own leadership s'more, so to speak:

S—spirit
M—mission
O—organization
R—relationship

These four **S-M-O-R** elements are central to the life and function of any organization, whether it be a small-group Bible study, an organized church, or a corporation like General Electric.[16]

- **S**pirit speaks to the anointing and attitude of the ministry group, including its energy and vision.
- **M**ission points to the outreach purpose of that ministry and answers the question, "Why are we here?"
- **O**rganization defines the management structure, including who is leading and what they're doing.
- **Re**lationship refers to the people networks and care functions within the ministry group.

In the life cycle of a ministry, **S**pirit (**S**) and **R**elationship (**R**) are usually strong in the beginning stages. For instance, when a small-group Bible study starts or a new church is planted, there's a strong sense that God is doing something great (**S**) and the people love being on this new adventure together (**R**). As the group matures, all four areas (**S-M-O-R**) come into their full expressions as organizational systems mature and mission becomes clearer. This is where every healthy ministry wants to be.

But with time, the forces of decline set in without rebirthing points. **S**pirit (**S**) and **R**elationship (**R**), the two factors that energized the early stages of the ministry, are usually the first to decline. Group gatherings become routine and people start to take each other for granted. Then a sense of **M**ission (**M**) gradually disappears. Group members lose touch with any reason for being other than to take care of themselves. Finally, with little left other than the lifeless mechanics of the **O**rganization (**O**), death sets in.

To avoid this, the four **S-M-O-R** components each need to be influenced, or guided, in ways that lead to regular rebirth and renewal. In their book, *Managing the Congregation*, Shawchuck and Heuser help us with two observations:[17]

1. We manage all four components as ministry leaders. I have found this very helpful in simplifying how I understand my core oversight responsibilities as a leader. Ministry can have a lot of tentacles to it, and churches tend to be rather sophisticated, complex, interactive organisms. But every day, when I get up, I know that I really only have four things to concentrate on as a leader: the group's **S**pirit, its **M**ission, its **O**rganization and its **R**elationships. The plan to do that need not be complicated, but managing those four areas is the leadership task. Staying focused on them and not getting distracted is the leadership challenge.

2. Changing one component will change the other three as well. All four of the **S-M-O-R** components actually interact with each other like a system. A key premise of systems theory is that a change to one component will ultimately bring change to the other system components as well.

When I became the pastor of Central Assembly, the congregation wanted to do more outreach in the neighborhoods immediately surrounding the church. Central was a strong world missions church, and my predecessor, Dr. David Watson, had fostered a wonderful heart for reaching out to lost people. It was clear to me that "mission" (**M**) was the **S-M-O-R** component I needed to emphasize during my first year there.

Adjusting the mission (**M**), however, turned out to affect the whole of the church's life. Our first outreach to the middle school next door catalyzed a markedly new spirit (**S**) in the church. At one point, as some of those new junior high students participated in one of our Sunday services, I sensed a release in the spiritual realm as it seemed like Jesus smiled on us. The outreach programs that began to flourish from that point on also brought noticeable changes to both our organizational systems (**O**) and our relational networks (**R**). New people stepped into leadership and people who didn't know each other began to connect for the first time on outreach teams.

In short, a purposeful adjustment to **M** brought growth in the **S, O,** and **R** dimensions of the church's life as well. These four ministry components, by God's design, are inseparable. Our role as leaders is to steward, or manage, them. We do so in strategic, God-directed ways as we listen to the Holy Spirit, assess the needs of the ministries we lead, and discern which of the four **S-M-O-R** components need to be prioritized at any given time. We can anticipate, however, that change in one component will bring change in the other three as well.

A Team Planning Exercise

What follows is an example of how you can use these four key leadership components in a strategic planning exercise. I have included two suggested assessment questions for each of the four **S-M-O-R** areas. These constitute a possible starting point, although the specific questions may change from one ministry to another. The goal is to eventually discern which of the four ministry elements most needs "rebirthing."

Because it's often difficult for us as leaders to see beyond our blind spots and personal perspectives, let me suggest that you answer these questions with a group of key team members and ministry influencers—combined with prayer, fasting, and a listening ear to the Holy Spirit. The answers may require both humility and courage, but the process can lead to intentional next-steps to transform the ministry you lead.

> **Spirit . . . Anointing and Vision**
> What has God been saying to us recently?
> What might be holding back God's Spirit among us?
>
> **Mission . . . Outreach and Results**
> Who are we to reach and retain?
> What strengths do we have to bring to that task?
>
> **Organization . . . Structure and Leaders**
> Are the right people doing the right things?
> How can we enhance our financial resources?

Relationship... Networks and Care
How are people personally caring for one another?
What is our pathway for new people?

CHAPTER 5

Strategic Process

*"Speaking the truth in love, we will grow to become in every respect
the mature body of him who is the head, that is, Christ."*
EPHESIANS 4:15

At the heart of it all, as ministry leaders we take the initiative to oversee and manage the spiritual, missional, organizational, and relational components of the ministry we lead. We do so in partnership with Christ, the ultimate church-builder, as we remain dependent on the Holy Spirit.

What does that look like in terms of specific, strategic leadership tasks that move people and ministries forward? Let me overview the answer with seven two-word phrases that, together, comprise a ministry grid or ministry philosophy, if you will. Associated with each statement are two key implementing words as well as the key underlying question each step addresses.

We *Model Servanthood*: Looking and Listening (Why do I lead?)

As leaders we are servants to the spiritual potential of those around us. One Sunday the obvious thought struck me. *People don't come to church so I can preach, as fulfilling as that is, but I get to preach so that the people who do come will be equipped to take another step forward in being all that Christ has called them to be.* In other words, I serve their potential.

Although leadership strategies generally start with casting vision (the third step below), true ministry leadership really begins with thinking and acting like a servant. If people become convinced that we as leaders are there for *them*, and not for ourselves, there will be no need for manipulation or control in order to have influence in their lives. How can people not want to follow someone who loves them and has their best interests at heart?

> **Like Jesus, as true spiritual leaders we need to focus on lifting up and adding value to the people around us—not using them to meet our own needs.**

Our motivations will profoundly affect our approach to leadership. We should never lead because we need to be needed or because we're dependent on the stimulation and ego reinforcement that leadership can give us. Neither should we lead for reasons of pay, position, popularity, privilege, or pride. Self-serving motivations will eventually betray our credibility as leaders. Instead, like Jesus, as true spiritual leaders we need to focus on lifting up and adding value to the people around us—not using them to meet our own needs.

This puts ministry leaders in the posture of always *looking* and *listening*. We always observe what is taking place around us and we look for ways to leave individuals and ministries better than when we first met them. We also listen more than we talk—a helpful but challenging discipline for people with natural leadership gifts. And in spite of our positions or titles, we pick up paper off the floor, help stack chairs after meetings, and give people time even when we would rather go home.

We *Set Attitudes*: Hoping and Honoring (What are my anxieties?)

Attitudes are contagious. I've often said to the staff members and volunteer leaders I've worked with that before we lead in behavior, we lead in attitude. If a certain group has a bad attitude, I may give them the benefit of the doubt for a while, but eventually I'll look to the leader. People catch our attitudes. Probably the biggest leadership mistake I ever made was to tolerate bad attitudes simply because the leaders were good at what they did. It would have been better to cut them loose than to let them stay around and poison the atmosphere.

After right motivation, leaders need right attitude. As ministry leaders we are relentlessly *hopeful* for the future, full of faith ourselves while engendering faith and confidence in those around us. We are also honoring of people. New visitors are not viewed as a threat, but a delight. People with problems are not dreaded, but embraced. And without being needlessly naïve, we trust people before we suspect them.

Dealing with our attitudes forces us to face our own anxieties. Can we stay non-anxious in spite of the uncertainty and anxiety around us? In leadership theory this is known as self-differentiation—the inner strength that keeps us from needlessly caving in to everyone else's fears and negative attitudes.[18] Biblically, we know this trait as *faith* with *courage*. Being a non-anxious leader doesn't make us insensitive to people or unwilling to make adjustments to our plans, but it does keep us focused on the mission and free from the need to always please people. This, in turn, fosters a sense of security and stability in the majority of those who follow us.

We *Cast Vision*: Communicating and Connecting (Where are we going?)

Because vision is a "visual" word, to *cast a vision* is to describe in some way a picture of the future. We are at point A right now, but God's Spirit has more for us than staying at point A. To simply keep point A maintained and in good condition would be called *transactional* leadership. But we understand that there is always a point B out there in our future if Jesus is at work in us. Vision describes what that point B could look like. To get there requires a *transformational* style of leadership that builds on two essential components:

> **1. A commitment to mission over maintenance**—We serve people's needs, but we refuse to stop there. We are always putting in front of people a compelling mission that is outside of us and bigger than any one of us. A vision, then, is a description of what things would look like a few years from now if we actually worked together to fulfill that mission.
>
> **2. A connection of vision to values**—If the vision we cast doesn't connect to anything people feel is important, they'll simply ignore it. Yet we must avoid the tendency to prematurely judge people if they don't immediately buy into the vision. Instead, we start with the assumption that somewhere, deep down, people want to see Christ's kingdom grow, their lives improve, and their contributions make a difference. Validate that assumption, and then link everything in the picture of a better future (vision) to those desires (values).

Then communicate the vision over and over. The old leadership adage still holds true: When we're tired of hearing ourselves talk about the vision, most people are just starting to notice. Communicate verbal pictures of the future. Highlight the life stories of people whose lives and ministries today are starting to look like what the future could hold for everyone. Avoid merely talking about good intentions that never seem to materialize, but keep reminding people of what they can become in Christ. And, if possible, use tangible symbols to keep a picture of that future in front of people.

When I was the pastor of Newport-Mesa Christian Center in

Southern California, the Lord gave me a picture of our future in the form of a carving I ran across in a Bethlehem souvenir shop on a trip to Israel. It was of the two spies returning from the Promised Land carrying a pole on their shoulders with a huge cluster of grapes hanging from it. We made a large reproduction of the grape cluster, hung it on a pole, and kept it on our church platform for over a year. As we launched out in our next steps of faith as a congregation, this was our vision of a future that would be met with God's provision, His abundance, and His divine favor.

We *Develop People*: Equipping and Encouraging (Are people growing and serving?)

Too many leaders spend most of their energies showcasing their own giftedness while leaving others dependent on them. But leading people somewhere means equipping them for ministry and encouraging their potential.

Unfortunately, I was a pastor for many years before I thought through what I wanted people to look like if they participated in the life of the congregation and listened to me preach every week for five years. Without doing that, I was preaching and

> "What do I want the people I pastor to look like in five years?"

leading with no specific developmental goals in mind for the people. My applications were weak, and people got tired of being told in some vague, directionless sort of way that they still weren't making the mark. I needed to balance "inspiration" with "application."

Because Jesus wants His church to *grow* up into His likeness, I took the word **G-R-O-W** as a way of answering that question, "What do I want the people I pastor to look like in five years?" I put what follows in the Sunday bulletin every week and taught it at every new member class.

Generous hearted—As stewards of our time, our talents, and our treasures, we seek to be people who serve wholeheartedly, give unselfishly, and care sacrificially. *We want to be known for what we give away, not what we take for ourselves—and we want to do it with joy.*

Relationally connected—Recognizing the God-given need for loving relationships, we seek to be involved in committed friendships and families, networked small groups, and effective ministry teams. *We want to be a place where people are more important than programs and relationships are more important than events.*

Outwardly focused—Given the great need in our world for people to know Christ and experience His loving power, we seek to be the kind of church that does not exist for itself. *We want to be a church whose direction is decided by our mission to reach people, not our personal preferences.*

Worship centered—Because we were created by God's hand to live for His glory, we seek lifestyles full of the Holy Spirit, honoring God in both purity and praise. *We want to be people for whom encountering God's presence is more important than merely being entertained.*

Each of these four areas could, in turn, have specific discipleship goals associated with them from year to year. But as I gave leadership to the spiritual, missional, organizational, and relational dimensions of the church, and as I preached from week to week, **G-R-O-W** gave me a sense of direction for applying the gospel to people's individual lives and developing the life of the fellowship as a whole.

We *Share Authority*: Enlisting and Empowering (Who are the leaders?)

Next to praying and having faith, getting the right people doing the right things is our hardest work. Yet when it happens, ministries transform. Experience has shown that increasing the volunteer leaders in a church from 5–7 percent to 12–15 percent of all active adherents will noticeably catalyze the growth of the church, in part because it increases the ministry capacity of the church far beyond that of a paid pastor and a few overworked volunteers.

Early in my ministry I heard the empowering process summarized in this simple but very helpful way:

- I do it and you watch;
- I do it and you help;
- You do it and I help;
- You do it and I watch.[19]

> **We need to march our insecurities to the cross and, at some point, trust people and give them responsibility.**

If our insecurities are going to kick in anywhere, it's probably here. Sharing leadership with others is a step that many ministry leaders ultimately find too difficult to take. It's so easy to fall prey to our self-protecting instincts and feel threatened by the strong people around us. But what if we actually worked to increase the leadership capacity of those around us, and hence the leadership capacity of the whole ministry? Our influence would multiply far beyond us. We wouldn't just be surrounded with helpers but with people who are truly "ministers."

We need to march our insecurities to the cross and, at some point, trust people and give them responsibility. Their leadership ability won't grow without it. Even if we've been burned in the past, we must resolve to get past doing ministry "to" people and start doing ministry "through" people. That is the Jesus way.

Here are three critical steps:

1. ENLIST

Recruiting potential ministry leaders takes more than a Sunday morning announcement. Personal phone calls, constant interactions with people in the church lobby, and a good-sized lunch budget all need to be part of the plan. Listen to people's hearts first, and then match their passions and dreams up with the next steps they could take toward leadership. Put a time frame on the commitment and begin by making them an assistant leader first, if possible.

2. EMPOWER

The key here is to delegate *authority*, not just *tasks*. If we assign tasks without giving people the authority (including resources) to fulfill those tasks, we set them up for failure. Make the responsibilities clear, but also the degree to which you trust them to make decisions, spend money, and teach others. Then coach them and let them try. Resist the temptation to dis-empower them by going behind their backs and doing the job for them.

3. SUPPORT

This is the follow-through to empowerment. Once someone steps into a leadership position, don't disappear on them. Leadership support teams provide mutual support and ongoing pastoral connection to novice leaders. Those leadership team meetings need to be priorities on our calendars. Answer leaders' emails and texts in a timely way, initiate phone calls to them, and pray for them a lot.

We *Require Excellence*: Inspecting and Improving (Are we fulfilling our mission?)

Excellence isn't to be confused with perfection. Perfection only frustrates people. But in any ministry group, someone has to set the bar for what are acceptable and unacceptable standards of performance. Is it fine for a small group leader to not show up to a meeting without notifying anyone? Should budgets be adhered to? Could lifestyle issues potentially require a leader to step down? What about incompetence? In all of these cases, and a myriad of others, it's ultimately the leader's responsibility to set the standards and call out the best in others.

Some of our most painful moments in leadership come when we need to have the difficult conversation with someone who isn't meeting acceptable standards. At those moments we need both wisdom *and* courage from the Holy Spirit. But we must also realize that avoiding confrontation has consequences of its own. Christ's mission is at stake, and a lot of other people can be negatively impacted if we do nothing. Sometimes we end up hurting the whole to protect the one, or ourselves.

When those awkward conversations do become necessary, my general rule of thumb is: confront with questions and coach with suggestions. If we start by confronting with accusations—like "you really blew it" or "you have a rebellious spirit" or "you're no good at this"—we'll hurt people and put up walls. But if we ask open questions aimed at helping people evaluate how they feel about what they're doing, we create a more disarming place from which to coach next steps—even if the suggestion is to step down.

Along the way I've also learned that we generally shouldn't confront people we have no intention of following through with. In short, deal with others like you would want to be dealt with yourself. Listen first, avoid expecting more of others than you do of yourself, and be willing to make tough decisions.

We *Show Appreciation*: Validating and Valuing (Are we celebrating people?)

These seven leadership steps get a little more technical as they progress, especially when it comes to equipping, empowering, and evaluating (numbers four, five, and six). But I often tell leaders that the starting place is simply doing number one and number seven really well. If people come to believe that we are there for them and not for ourselves (servanthood), and if we validate and value them (appreciation), we'll have immense influence in their lives. People will *want* to follow us.

I personally have little felt need to write hand-written notes, but as a leader I force myself to do it as a way of expressing appreciation to people. One Sunday I noticed one of our members serving in some way, so on Monday I wrote him a thank-you note. A few days later I got a letter back from him thanking me for my note and telling me that he was thinking about framing it. Why? Because he had been serving voluntarily in that ministry for eleven years, but I was the first one to ever thank him.

As leaders we may need to give up counting our own thank-you notes but, when it comes to those we lead, it's totally unacceptable that any of them should feel unappreciated. We should be people's biggest encouragers and their most vocal cheerleaders. We need to constantly see potential in people, verbalize appreciation for them, and affirm their efforts. Those we lead are hungry to know we value them and we recognize the difference they make. That, more than criticism, sets the tone for bringing out the best in others and helping them excel. That's when leadership becomes pure joy.

CHAPTER 6

Staffing Criteria

"Ask the Lord of the harvest, therefore, to send out workers into his harvest field."
MATTHEW 9:38

If getting the right people doing the right things is some of our most important work as leaders, how do we find the *right people*?

Few leadership decisions are more consequential than the choice of who is or is not on our leadership team. A wrong decision can take a long time to fix, but a right decision can take a ministry area to new levels of fruitfulness. The leaders around us determine the leadership capacity of the ministry as a whole, and therefore the degree to which it can grow and achieve its mission. Ministries generally cannot grow past their leadership capacity.

For a church to break the 200 barrier, the primary pastoral leader will need to equip and empower a leadership team to work alongside him or her, as described in the previous chapter. Similarly, some churches may not break the 700 barrier, or the infamous 2,000 barrier, until some sort of staffing change takes place that replaces those whose leadership capacities have maxed out with those *harder-to-find* individuals with the God-given ability to lead the church beyond those ceilings.

Selecting the right leaders is holy work. We are partnering with God who calls people. From my thirty years of pastoral experience I've developed a set of criteria, both intentional and intuitive, for helping me find the mind of the Lord when it comes to selecting people. These criteria can be used for selecting key volunteer leaders or hiring paid staff, although the requirements would be more rigorous for paid staff.

I pose the sixteen requirements as questions that I seek to find the answer to either verbally or nonverbally. I consider the first three questions the most important: (1) spiritual maturity, (2) developed character, and (3) right motives. Only after I have sufficient information about these three do I move on to skills and team fit.

1. *Is there authentic spirituality behind your ministry performance?*

We can't assess leadership capacity without talking about the anointing of the Holy Spirit. Too often, in leadership selection, we overlook the spiritual anointing that one walks in, backed by a lifestyle of walking in intimacy with the Lord. But moving ministry forward must always be about a person's ability to stay in step with what the Spirit is doing and doing it in His power. We are looking for more than talent.

One of the ways I try to discern this, in addition to direct questions about the person's personal spiritual life, is to create an opportunity to hear the person pray out loud. It tells me a lot about the person's heart and whether they truly seem to "abide in Christ" as a lifestyle.

2. *Are you someone I would want others to be like?*

A good leadership self-test is to ask ourselves, "Would I want others to look like me when it comes to my character, my

> **Who people are is far more influential than what people do.**

spirituality, my attitudes, and my priorities?" The equivalent for parents would be, "Do I want my kids to turn out like me?" For the leaders we bring close around us, the question is no different.

Spiritual formation and life learning take more than a classroom experience. They require personal modeling and formational relationships. Who people are is far more influential than what people do. We therefore need to select leaders whose godliness we would want others to emulate—leaders who embody what we want our future ministry to look like.

3. *What ministries have you done without pay or position?*

This question has an objective answer to it, but it gives a glimpse into the less obvious motivational structure of a person's life. Does this person have enough love for Jesus and passion for ministry that they were willing to serve even when there was no position or pay? If the answer is no, then they likely do not belong in a paid pastoral staff role. What we do voluntarily is what reveals our true colors.

For potential volunteer leaders, the question would be similar. Have they served in the past without needing a lot of convincing or recognition? Have they shown initiative on their own to seek out ministry involvement, or do they serve only when someone asks them? Past performance is usually a good predictor of future behavior in this area and can yield valuable insight into motivational patterns.

4. *Are you an effective communicator, interpersonally and publicly?*

Being able to connect and communicate with other people is essential to the full range of interpersonal interactions a leader needs to navigate. Leaders influence and motivate others, in part, by being able to articulate truth, communicate information, verbalize expectations, express appreciation, confront issues, and empathize with the feelings of others—all without leaving people needlessly hurt or offended.

Certainly this is one of the most complex skills in a leader's arsenal. Trying to assess a potential leader's proficiency at this can happen, in part, by simply listening to them talk. Often when we are recruiting new leaders, we make the mistake of doing most of the talking. Instead, we should listen and look for that person's ability to connect and engage with us. Are they conversational? Do they look you in the eye? Can they read your mood and intent? Do they have an accurate sense as to how they come across to you and others?

5. *What are you really good at?*

For both effectiveness and longevity, ministry assignments must eventually line up with the person's primary anointing and ability. The key is not only finding the right person, but eventually getting that person doing the right things. Those right things will obviously need to align closely with the person's primary giftedness.

> The key is not only finding the right person, but eventually getting that person doing the right things.

Explore roles the person has filled in the past that others have responded well to. What do people who are close to them perceive as their strengths and how closely do those strengths line up with their passions? Good reference work will be important here to determine if there's a gap between strengths the person perceives and strengths that others perceive.

Unfortunately, in spite of our best efforts, what a person is fully capable of isn't always immediately obvious. Sometimes it's important simply to get talented people on our team and let their specific roles sort themselves out later.

6. *Can you think for yourself or will I have to think for you?*

Every person being considered for a staff or volunteer leadership assignment will have to make their own decision as to whether or not they want to work with a supervising leader who does most of the thinking for them. Not everyone, especially stronger leaders, can work under highly controlling styles of leadership without feeling devalued and distrusted.

Empowering-focused, secure team leaders, on the other hand, give room for good people to run. In that kind of environment potential new leaders need to possess an ability to think within the parameters of the mission, initiate new ideas, and contribute creatively to the whole. They also need to be able to take responsibility for their mistakes, understand accountability, and respect the authorities that they will be working under.

7. *Are you lazy or do you have a strong work ethic and personal stamina?*

Can the person stay focused even when they don't find a required task particularly interesting? Are they motivated more by what they feel like doing or by a sense of responsibility? Do they have a history of working hard, and have they ever been influenced by a person with a strong work ethic? Hard work isn't an old fashioned idea; lazy people on the team will drag everyone else down.

On the other side of that coin is the issue of stamina. Have they developed the ability to handle fatigue and cope with stress? Does their health allow them to keep up with the demands of the proposed leadership role? What have they done to stay emotionally and physically healthy?

8. *Do you attract and endear people to you or do you create conflict?*

One of the paradoxes of spiritual leadership is that we are to please God, not people. Yet for a leader to be effective, people need to be drawn to that person in a pleasing, respectful way. Ministry leaders who empower others generally have winsome personalities. They also know how to help people work together peacefully and in good will. Their personalities and leadership styles don't breed needless conflict.

As with the previous question, honest references from people they have worked with previously is a better metric than the potential leader's self-perception, which in these areas tends not to be objective if there are problems.

9. *Can you minister "through" people as well as "to" people?*

At issue here is a whole philosophy of ministry, not to mention a skill set. Second Timothy 2:2 prescribes a reproducing ministry strategy in which leaders invest in other leaders who can, in turn, equip others. My friend and experienced campus pastor, Brady Bobbink, would often call this "Second Timothy 2:2'ing it to the world."

> **Leaders who reproduce themselves have a heart to develop people and a willingness to share authority with others.**

We expect leaders to reproduce leaders. For pastoral staff positions in larger ministries, this becomes an essential role. Leaders in those settings need to preach, teach, organize, and accomplish tasks while allocating time to equip others to do the same. Listen to potential leaders talk for a while and it will become clear whether they have an instinct for ministering "'through" as well as "to." Leaders who reproduce themselves have a heart to develop people and a willingness to share authority with others.

10. *Are you able to spot leaders and motivate volunteers?*

If equipping people for ministry is an important priority, this question naturally flows out of the previous one. Good leaders develop an eye for seeing potential in others. They believe in what God can do through people, they encourage people to step up to it, and then they help people succeed. Along the way they also develop an intuitive sense as to who is ready to start that journey.

What experience does this person have recruiting volunteers and identifying potential leaders? Can they cast a vision and motivate without manipulating? How would they approach training, equipping, and oversight? Have previous leaders invested in them in that way?

11. *Can you be constructively critical without being cynical?*

The Achille's heel of being astute, observant, and idealistic can be the tendency to also be cynical. Cynicism is the toxic blend of both a critical eye and a mistrusting spirit. It ultimately leaves us powerless, unable to believe that there's hope for institutions or authority structures of any kind, including ministry organizations. If the pain of broken trust isn't dealt with at some point in our lives, we become its victims.

How has this person worked through past disappointments with other people, especially authority figures? Have they developed a wounded spirit over time? How do they feel about their parents? How do they view larger denominational structures, and what is their understanding of accountability? How do they interact with people who don't agree with them philosophically? Are they self-aware enough to distinguish the difference between critical thinking and cynicism in their own lives and how that would work out on a team?

12. *Are you able to be respectfully loyal to your senior leader(s)?*

To work willingly and well on another person's team obviously requires respect and loyalty. Imagine working for someone you don't respect, or being on a team of people you don't trust. On the other hand, perhaps out of their own insecurities, supervising leaders sometimes read disloyalty into every mistake or the first hint of someone questioning their decisions.

As complicated as this issue can be in both directions, past history is probably the best indicator. Has the prospective leader had a history of being repeatedly dissatisfied with their supervisors? If so, are they aware that some of the issues may be their own? How have they worked through that? And most importantly, what are their specific expectations of supervising leaders?

13. *Can you manage your own money as well as a ministry budget?*

Jesus related financial management to the qualifications for ministry responsibility. "So if you have not been trustworthy in handling worldly wealth, who will trust you with true riches" (Luke 16:11)? For ministry leaders, this is an important issue. Whether large or small, most ministries have some sort of resource budget that needs to be developed and managed.

If a person is weak at financial management, determine first whether it's a character problem involving wastefulness, out of control spending, or some other lack of personal discipline as opposed to simple inattention to administrative details or lack of training. Then spell out clearly the budget management expectations, describe where the person can find help, and be clear about the consequences of persistent overspending.

14. *Do you have "bounce-back-ability," and can you cope with criticism?*

Unfortunately, leadership can be brutal. We are asking people to take on a role that will subject them to disappointment and, likely, personal criticism. Invariably they'll get hurt emotionally at some point. They may also face physical and spiritual exhaustion. The question is whether a leader has developed, at least at basic levels, the necessary coping skills to keep going.

> Whenever we put a person into leadership, we are inherently making a commitment to stand with them and help them succeed.

Whenever we put a person into leadership, we are inherently making a commitment to stand with them and help them succeed. We commit to trust them until proven wrong, especially when we hear complaints about them from other people. New leaders always benefit from being assured up front that we won't abandon them during hard times or arbitrarily throw them under the bus in order to protect ourselves.

15. *Are you confident without being cocky and humble without being insecure?*

Cockiness and insecurity are, of course, the counterfeits of true confidence and humility. In Galatians 2:20 Paul described himself as being *"crucified with Christ,"* so that *"I no longer live, but Christ lives in me."* This is where true confidence and humility spring from, freeing us to live out our "in Christ" identity and move forward with what the Lord has called us to do.

The litmus test of Christ-centered confidence and humility is the ability truly to care for and love other people. We may be called to lead, but ultimately we are called to love. Nothing can replace that in the life of a prospective leader. Pay attention to attitude and try to get a handle on whether they are seeking a leadership position for ego or out of a sense of entitlement or because of a true desire to grow others and to honor Jesus.

16. *Can you fit with the culture of this ministry and its staff/leadership team?*

Some personnel search models focus on character, competence, and chemistry. This would be the "chemistry" question. How might this person stretch and add value to the existing leadership team without tearing it apart? Is there a compatible fit between this person and who we are, or want to be, as a ministry?

When I interviewed people for pastoral staff positions, I generally had the existing staff pastors take the candidate out to lunch *without* me. I had already encouraged the candidate to ask the staff any question he or she had about working on the team and under my oversight. Later I debriefed with staff, looking for two things: (1) their general feedback about the person and, most importantly, (2) their sense as to whether this person would fit on our team culture.

Three Concluding Perspectives

First, these questions are guidelines for selecting *leader*s in particular, not volunteers in general. There are those who serve and those who, with a servant's heart, also lead. Biblically the qualifications for leadership are higher for leaders. So are the responsibilities and demands.

Second, this evaluative grid is long and shouldn't suggest that you need to achieve a seemingly unattainable standard of perfection before putting someone into leadership. Many of us have done most of our growing *because* of the demands of leadership, not prior to them.

Third, the qualifications and subsequent accountability will understandably be higher for full-time, paid pastoral staff members than for volunteer leaders who may give just a handful of hours per month to program leadership. It's easy to make the demands of leadership feel unattainable to people with families, full-time jobs, and friendship networks. But if roles and expectations are clearly spelled out and mentoring support is provided, volunteer leaders can often carry the majority of the leadership roles in a church.

SECTION 3

Skills and Strengths

At twenty-six I was completing nine years of education in aerospace engineering. I had to decide whether to become the full-time pastor of the campus ministry I had been leading as a student, or pursue an engineering career when I graduated. My academic advisor had assured me that I could get a good engineering job anywhere in the country that I wanted to live. Yet I felt the call to stay at the university after graduation and pastor the campus ministry full time.

The call into vocational ministry won out. Having since watched others work through similar decisions, here are some questions I've come to appreciate. The last one focuses on the development of three key skills that will be the focus of this next section.

Should You Go Into Full Time Ministry?

- ☐ Is there is a persistent conviction in your heart, tested over time, that you are to do this?
- ☐ Do you feel released from where you are now and would you be changing careers for the right reasons?

- ☐ Could you be happy doing something other than vocational ministry?
- ☐ Are you ready to love a group of people and personally sacrifice for their benefit?
- ☐ Do you have a distracting passion for what you think a local congregation could accomplish?
- ☐ Are you willing to take calls in the middle of the night and spend part of your days in hospitals?
- ☐ Do you have the heart to manage budgets, develop resources, and perhaps take a pay cut?
- ☐ Is your self-identity developed enough that you'll be able to handle criticism and disappointment without over-reacting?
- ☐ Have you dealt with your insecurities to the point that you could empower others and not be intimidated by having strong people around you?
- ☐ Are your work habits strong enough that you could stay focused and on task without a lot of direct supervision from day to day?
- ☐ Are you willing to keep growing your skills as a team-builder, communicator, and change agent?

CHAPTER 7

Team Building

"He appointed twelve that they might be with him and that he might send them out to preach."
MARK 3:14

One of my greatest joys as a ministry leader has been working with the wonderful teams of associate pastors and volunteer leaders the Lord has put around me over the years. These teams often constituted some of my most valued friendship circles. I would regularly feel the strength of *their* strengths around me and learned to be nervous when people more gifted than me weren't around. We would dream together, plan together, pray together, do mission together, and drink too much coffee together.

Jesus was a remarkable team builder, and He understood the power of "together." Midway through His ministry, He called twelve of His followers to be close-in on an amazing "learner to leader" journey. Along the way, He implanted vision (Matt. 4:19), built character (Matt. 5–7), and taught skills (Matt. 10).

After Jesus ascended into heaven, these same leaders-in-the-making took steps to ensure the ongoing integrity of their team by filling an unfortunate vacancy in their ranks (Acts 1), after which Jesus baptized them in the Holy Spirit (Acts 2). Everything came together at that point, and, not surprisingly, they stayed *together* as a leadership team, overseeing the burgeoning life of the early church and working together to raise up more leaders.

Effective ministry leaders learn the skills of team building. None of us can fulfill our callings alone. Neither do we want to lead Christ's church in carelessly isolated ways. Getting people to work with us and with each other to advance the life and mission of the church is at the heart of ministry leadership. If we build ministries that are little more than one-man-shows confined to our own ministry capacities, we've missed the Jesus way and have put a lid on the ministries we lead.

If the ministries we lead are in crisis mode, needing "emergency room" intervention, then someone will need to step in, take charge, and unilaterally make changes in order to "save the patient," so to speak. But to lead that way for the long term would probably kill the patient. The healthier a ministry is, the more other people will be involved in participatory, partnering ways. Healthy ministries develop biblical, people-centered, team-based approaches to ministry.

As for team builders themselves, their greatest joy is the success of the people around them. They get over the insecurities that make them either too self-protecting or too self-promoting and come to honestly believe that the success of their team members is their own success. The stronger the people around them, the happier they are. Good team builders derive some of their deepest satisfaction from doing ministry *through* people, not just *to* people.

T-E-A-M Functioning

There are a number of approaches to this particular formulation, but I like to summarize the essential elements of team functioning in this way:

> **T**—trust
> **E**—encouragement
> **A**—accountability
> **M**—mission

In highly functioning teams, all four factors are strong. They are also peer-to-peer reinforced, not just leader-driven. There's enough *trust* on the team that members give each other the benefit of the doubt and create a culture that can tolerate taking risks together. The role of each member is not only spelled out, but regularly *encouraged* and affirmed by the other team members. Likewise, individual *accountability* is not just to the team leader but to everyone on the team. And *mission,* defined as the purposes and goals of the team, is embraced or owned by everyone.

> **If mission determines what a team does, values describe how the team does it.**

These are the four characteristics of healthy teamwork. Nurturing them, however, is the process of living out predefined values that guide how the team actually functions from day to day. The team leader will guide in defining those values and developing alignment with them.

If mission determines *what* a team does, values describe *how* the team does it. Values act like guardrails around the mission and shape the convictions that guide team behavior. Vision, then, is a picture of the future if the mission and values were lived out. But at the heart of it all are the values. They spell out the process steps for building team health.

A number of years ago I wrote down ten values that have guided my own building of teams. Writing the values out made them definable and actionable. Team core values may vary from team to team, but here are mine:

Ten Core Values for a Ministry Team

1. *Prayer and scriptural principles undergird everything we do.*
2. *There are no superstars on the team, only humble servant-leaders who are working toward personal effectiveness and the success of other team members.*

3. *Lay volunteers don't work for us—we serve them, setting attitude and helping them to achieve their in-Christ potential.*
4. *Honest, personal feedback and evaluation are expected and valued parts of our lives as growing people.*
5. *Feedback concerning the church's ministry, both positive and negative, can be shared freely and safely among us.*
6. *We work through conflicts with other team members rather than avoiding them, always willing to risk trust by extending the benefit of the doubt to one another.*
7. *Priority attention is given to personal family commitments and spiritual disciplines.*
8. *Time is budgeted and wisely managed to accomplish timeless results.*
9. *Hard work, initiative, and innovation are valued over functionally maintaining the status quo.*
10. *We strive for excellence, combined with anointing, in everything we do.*

These values, working in tandem with each other, lay out a practical pathway for nurturing T-E-A-M strength. Once a year I would review this entire list with my primary ministry teams. The rest of the year I would stay focused on situational opportunities to reinforce the values one or two at a time—in staff meetings, one-on-one conversations, or those spontaneous teaching moments every leader looks for. I would usually take opportunity to affirm specific team behaviors when they aligned with our values. Or I would occasionally use the team values as a doorway to correct unhelpful behavior.

It's one thing to have values, however, and another to enforce and reinforce them. It takes courage to lead well. My tendency to want to be the nice guy would sometimes sap my courage when I should have stepped up to address an issue. And my reactions were sometimes not always predictable, which would keep my teams off-kilter. A trusted pastoral staff member once said to me, "You sometimes over-react to secondary issues but don't get upset enough about really important issues. It makes it hard for the team to focus on the right things."

Values need constant monitoring and reinforcing, which takes courage and consistency from the team leader. That means acting and reacting in the right ways.

Aggressive, Passive, or Assertive?

Both action and inaction have consequences. Instead of being too *aggressive* or too *passive*, effective team builders need to be appropriately *assertive*. Aggressiveness can turn into abuse, victimizing team members. Passivity, on the other hand, erodes trust in the team leader. It confuses expectations, sidesteps accountability, and jeopardizes the mission. I've heard horror stories from both camps—leaders who aggressively control, demean, and hurt team members and leaders who passively ignore team members, give no direction, and avoid addressing problems.

Assertiveness is decisive but respectful action. It's not heavy-handed and controlling, but neither is it hands-off and non-direct. A team leader's assertiveness can help team members feel valued, yet accountable; stretched, yet fulfilled. This, in turn, leads to the kinds of synergies that accomplish mission in remarkable ways.

Here are several core competencies that assertive team leaders can develop.

Core Competencies for Team Builders

An Ability to Foster Team Dependence on the Holy Spirit

The first and last of the Ten Core Values for a Ministry Team listed above address this issue. Praying and fasting together, insisting that strategy line up with biblical principles, and mentoring each team leader spiritually are all a part of the process. But

> **Excellence is important, but anointing reminds us that, at its best, excellence is not enough.**

most importantly, avoid the pitfall of elevating excellence over anointing. Excellence is our part, but anointing is God's part. In a very real sense the two are counter-intuitive. Excellence is important, but anointing reminds us that, at its best, excellence is not enough. I would often say to my pastoral teams, "Every day we are performing a marriage. Not a marriage between two people, but the marriage of excellence and anointing." This is stewardship *and* Spirit, not stewardship *or* Spirit.

An Ability to Lift Others Up

Good team builders often believe in those around them more than those persons believe in themselves. As discussed in chapter 3, a fundamental axiom of leadership is that people tend to rise to what they think their leaders see them to be. Helping people to see their potential and then becoming their biggest cheerleader is one of the most potent skills of team building.

To do this, team builders have what I call "pastoral eyes." In spite of what they may learn about people's failings and struggles, by God's grace they still see potential in them. Unlike solo leaders, team builders aren't preoccupied with their personal performance but with bringing out the best in others. They affirm and stretch their team members and then step out of the spotlight in order to let them step in. They use "we" language more than "me" language.

An Ability to Create Safe Interpersonal Environments

When teams aren't emotionally or relationally safe, dysfunction sets in. On unsafe teams, it's unlikely that people will risk being honest or forthcoming with each other or the team leader. It's a dangerous place to be when no one wants to tell the truth. In the

TEAM BUILDING

Ten Core Values for a Ministry Team listed above, honest feedback is valued and expected. A culture of safety makes this work.

As a team leader it was never easy for me to welcome critical feedback of either the ministry or of me. But my team members were the ones who knew me the best and the persons I trusted the most. I couldn't afford to insulate myself from their feedback or penalize them for telling me what I might not want to hear.

I also knew that if I had competent staff members, other organizations would try to recruit them. To accuse them of disloyalty for simply exploring options would have been antithetical to the culture of safety we were trying to build. I wanted them to be able to work through the discernment process with me, not without me. Although I did all of this imperfectly, I tried to make it safe for team members to engage me without the fear that they would pay a price for it later.

An Ability to Communicate Clearly and Consistently

Ask team members about the biggest problem with their teams and invariably they'll say "lack of communication." Communication problems plague most organizations, and team leaders are often the problem. In my case it was because I have a somewhat quiet personality. This made me a good listener but a poor communicator. Team members had to guess what I

> **Effective team-builders take the guesswork out of teamwork by being verbal, specific, and even repetitive.**

was thinking. I also assumed too much when it came to what I thought people knew.

Effective team-builders take the guesswork out of teamwork by being verbal, specific, and even repetitive. If they're natural talkers, they resist the tendency to talk about everything except what team members need to know. During discussions they may even ask what team members are hearing just to be sure everyone is on the same page. They also make sure that valued team members never hear a major directional announcement for the first time on a Sunday morning with everyone else.

It takes a surprising amount of work to keep everyone informed, but consistent communication systems will set team members up for success, help them feel affirmed, enhance their sense of ownership in the mission, and save them from the awkwardness of being caught in the dark in front of other people on important issues.

An Ability to Be Permission-Giving Rather Than Punitive

The natural follow-through to an environment of relational safety and healthy communication is a team culture that gives permission to people. As a pastor, I would often say that I had the ministry of saying yes—yes to people's dreams and callings. At times I had to say no, but generally it was better to encourage innovation and initiative, within the bounds of our shared mission, than to stifle it.

One particular pastoral team that I assumed leadership of seemed to be hesitant to take risks. I tried to push them, but an influential team member spoke up, "Pastor, you need to be patient with us. We aren't used to working with a permission-giving leader." Unfortunately, the team had been conditioned to a leadership environment where failures were punished. By contrast, permission-giving cultures let people take risks and live to tell about it. Otherwise team members default to self-protecting behaviors and very little moves forward.

An Ability to Inspect Without Disrespecting

A clever leadership adage states that, "People will *re*-spect what you *in*-spect." Accountability is essential to good team functioning. The problem is that there are both motivating and demotivating ways to inspect. Doing it in an untrusting, intrusive way can come across as demeaning, especially to other strong leaders. So good team leaders actually *coach* more than they *police.*

One of the most valuable supervision questions to ask team members can be, "What's the biggest challenge you are facing right now?" followed by, "Is there a way I can help?"

Beyond that,

- ☐ make expectations clear up front
- ☐ define agreed upon systems and metrics for accountability
- ☐ let people actually do what they are expected to do
- ☐ insist that team members admit and take responsibility for their mistakes

If there are persistent performance problems, address them. However, when possible, avoid shaming team members in front of each other. My rule of thumb was to affirm publicly but correct privately.

An Ability to Keep a Group On Mission

Teams exist to fulfill purposes and produce results. Unfortunately, activity can too easily be mistaken for productivity. Being busy and accomplishing the mission may be two very different things. More than putting in time, pulling off another event, or even feeling good about doing ministry, the mission always asks, "What did God do?" and, "What was accomplished that made a difference?"

Effective team leaders are relentless about results. They are the stewards of the team's mission, so they are constantly asking the "Why do this?" questions up front and the "What did it accomplish?" questions afterward. They're also courageous enough to ask what the team should *not* be doing in order to make room for what it should be doing. Planned neglect can be agonizing, but it's important for staying on mission.

Mission also needs to be factored into the structure of team meetings. Patrick Lencioni in his book, *Death by Meeting*,[20] points out that it's difficult for team members to keep switching back and forth in the same meeting between missionally strategic agenda items and administratively logistic ones. Better to separate weekly logistic meetings, where everyone participates in event planning and calendar coordination, from less frequent but highly important long term strategy meetings. Otherwise mission will be derailed by week to week administration.

We're better together, and it's amazing what we can accomplish in teams, with God's help. Jesus' model is ministry together. Where leaders bring people together and develop the skills needed to cultivate trust (**T**), encouragement (**E**), accountability (**A**) and mission (**M**), there can be the kind of teamwork that dynamically transforms lives, churches, communities, and nations.

CHAPTER 8

Public Speaking

"I give you this charge: Preach the word."
2 Timothy 4:1–2

Leaders communicate, and great leaders communicate well. In his fascinating book, *The Last Lion*, William Manchester quotes the remarkable twentieth-century orator and world leader, Winston Churchill, as saying that anyone who masters the skill of public speaking is in possession of the most precious of gifts. "He who enjoys it," Churchill said, "wields a power more durable than that of a great king. He is an independent force in the world."[21]

On the day of Pentecost, Jesus' followers were filled with the Holy Spirit. Something transformational and life impacting took place in their hearts as God's power flowed into them. Not surprisingly, they "began to speak in other tongues as the Spirit enabled them" (Acts 2:4). Speaking in tongues is a verbal evidence, supernatural in nature, reminding everyone that the Spirit is given to make us "witnesses" (Acts 1:8), to empower us to be God's mouthpiece to the world. Peter, who preached the first sermon of the Christian church, would later say, "If anyone speaks, they should do so as one who speaks the very words of God" (1 Peter 4:11). Paul charged Timothy: "Preach the word" (2 Tim. 4:2).

God's Spirit and verbal proclamation have always gone together, from the prophetic voices of the Old Testament to the great sermons and preachers of the New Testament, and now on to us. It's curious to note that Churchill believed the key to a speaker's impact was sincerity. "Before he can inspire them with any emotion he must be swayed by it himself.... Before he can move their tears his own must flow. To convince them he must himself believe."[22] As followers of Christ, this is what the Holy Spirit does for us. He fills us with Himself, our hearts become passionately engaged with His heart, His truth shapes our core convictions, and out of the overflow of that we speak, all by His power.

This makes communicating God's Word one of our most important priorities as spiritual leaders. According to 2 Timothy 3:16, "All Scripture is God-breathed and is useful for" . . .

> teaching—(what we need to believe)
> rebuking—(what we need to stop doing)
> correcting—(what we need to start doing)
> training—(what we need to become)

The result is what Paul described in the next verse, the very thing all of us want to see in the lives of those we serve: people equipped to fully obey and serve God. Preaching and teaching are central to serving the spiritual potential of those we minister to, whether in the context of smaller groups or in front of large crowds. An ability to communicate isn't an optional skill for ministry leaders.

Determining to Improve

For most of us, learning to speak well will probably be a lifelong quest. When it comes to public speaking, it's especially easy to fall into a kind of self-delusion, thinking we're better than we really

> For most of us, learning to speak well will probably be a lifelong quest.

are and people enjoy hearing us speak more than they really do. Unfortunately, what we sound like to ourselves isn't always how we come across to others.

At about the fifteen-year point in full-time ministry, I felt like I had stopped growing as a preacher and needed some help. So with the help of an associate pastor we put together a pulpit committee, for lack of a better name. The group included a high school girl, an eighty-three-year-old woman who was praying for revival, a college professor and his wife, a young couple with small children, a couple with teenagers, and a fifty-year-old single mom with grown children. We selected a cross-section of the people who listened to me every Sunday.

Each person had a half-page sheet they would fill out after the sermon and hand to me. There were four questions on it: "What was the theme of the message? What was the purpose of the message? What helped you hear this message well? What would have helped you hear this message better?" That last question was the painful one, although it also bothered me how often they could identify the theme of the message but not its purpose, meaning that the topic was clear but why they needed the message was not.

Once every three weeks we met together for an hour and a half on a Sunday afternoon. During the first forty-five minutes, we reviewed the previous three Sunday morning sermons. I had already seen their written evaluation sheets, but I needed the face-to-face feedback as well. They could say anything they wanted. It made me nervous, but people are rarely vicious when you intentionally ask for their input in a safe environment.

Their observations, both positive and negative, were just what I needed to help me communicate better. "Your introductions are too long." "How your main point applied to me wasn't clear." "That particular illustration didn't seem to fit the point you were making." "The sermon kept my attention, but it was hard to tell where you were going with it." and on it would go. It was a painful but loving gift to me.

During the second half of that hour-and-a-half meeting, we went over the Scripture texts I was planning on preaching over the next three Sundays. I wasn't asking them to write the sermons for me, but I felt I had been losing touch with the kinds of questions people have when they read the Scriptures. If I'm not addressing those questions and relating the text to real issues in their lives, then something is wrong. The committee members would share, from their perspective, what confused them and what stood out to them in the upcoming passages. Those Sunday afternoon encounters with the text became great Bible studies.

Our pulpit committee met every three weeks for a year. An unanticipated spin-off was that the committee members grew in their own ability to hear messages. "No one ever taught us how to listen to a sermon," they would say. But the benefit was mainly mine.

Developing Messages

My Smartphone and computer require periodic upgrades, as do many of the program applications they run. Here is an upgrade check list for effectively preparing and delivering messages. Look for two or three areas to work on improving over the next year.

- ☐ Try to increase sermon preparation time by 10 to 20 percent. If possible, give away a weekly responsibility to someone else in order to spend more time studying and praying. Few things matter more than communicating God's Word effectively.

- ☐ Focus on finding the *single thread* of truth that connects all the verses in the Scripture passage. Let this determine the singular purpose of the message. Try to express that one central truth in the message title. It's hard work, but simplify, simplify, simplify. This is not being simplistic. A truly focused message can actually be quite profound.

- After studying the passage, pray in the Spirit over both the text and the hearers. Ask the Holy Spirit to reveal to you specific applications. How does the truth of the text directly relate to the lives of the people who will be listening? In other words, message preparation requires that we exegete both the text and our audience.

- Right from the beginning stages of designing the message, remember that life-change preaching ultimately answers two questions: "What?" (explanation) and "So what?" (application). Try to aim at the *minds* of your listeners with the "What?" question, their *wills* with the "So what?" question, and their *emotions* as the message draws them in and leads them toward a response.

- Without making things complicated, develop the central truth of the passage in the form of a simple outline that follows the flow of the text. Stick to the one central truth, but divide the directional flow of the text into a few key steps that unfold and explain that central truth. Try to develop the message flow like a story line, one point leading naturally to the next.

- As much as possible, put verbs into your key points and relate them to real issues in people's lives as you walk through the text. In the words of well-known pastor Rick Warren, if application is the point of preaching, then "make your applications your points."[23] Try to avoid 95 percent exegetical content with 5 percent application thrown in at the end. Bring people's life situations into every main point of the flow of the message.

- Keep the applications practical, doable (not too vague or too many), and always related to the central truth. They should be both "life specific," in that they deal with the real issues people are facing, and "strategically actionable," in that they describe what people should actually do with the truth, and how. Specific applications take a lot of thought. They need to be much more specific and how-to oriented than simply some version of, "be more committed."

- [ ] Avoid meandering or including too many ideas. Go from beginning to conclusion in as straight a line as possible. Edit out digressions or tangents that don't relate to the central truth. After the first draft of the outline, be ruthless and prune, prune, prune! After years of preaching, I learned to take my nearly finalized outline and cut 25 percent of it out, forcing me to keep the message focused and true to its central purpose.

- [ ] Support every key point with the text itself. Try to avoid reading the Scripture at the beginning and never referring to it again. If some points don't relate directly to the text, prune some more. Make sure that both the content of Scripture and the circumstances of people's lives stay central throughout the message.

- [ ] Avoid making main points without illustrating them. Finding the right story, life illustration, visual aid, or applicable how-to can be time consuming... but invaluable. Pray for creativity. Constantly be looking for sermon illustrations in everyday situations, books, media, and personal life experiences.

- [ ] Word the key points to apply to people's lives *and* be interesting and memorable without being trite or inauthentic. Phrase the key focus of the message in a way that you can repeat throughout the message, and that people can remember.

PUBLIC SPEAKING

- ☐ Bring people's questions and life situations into the message right from the beginning. Creatively let people know up front why they should listen to you for the next thirty minutes. Then let the message build in interest through the use of *why* questions. For example, the *what* of the text is that God says to love people, but why would He want us to?

- ☐ As with any story line that engages people's attention and hearts, let the message unfold as a kind of story with tension, urgency, emotional connection, and finally resolution. Pace the tone and timing of the message with intensity, humor, pauses, and natural transitions between points.

- ☐ As a discipline, consider cutting the normal sermon delivery time by five to ten minutes, focusing on anointed impact rather than needless length. Allow more time for altar response. Aim for actionable applications and hearer responses that lead to an encounter with the Holy Spirit.

- ☐ While being applicable and practical, never forget to balance human responsibility with God's enabling grace. Keep elevating God's greatness and power. Don't compromise on sin but end with gospel-centered hope. Always take people to the cross of Christ, no matter what the topic or text.

- ☐ Be authentic in communicating the message. Avoid coming across as artificial or unnatural. Speak with passion and conviction, expressed with appropriate variations in tone of voice. Avoid being too monotone, or only yelling. Seek to connect with people at the level of their minds, emotions, and wills—not only in the content but in the style of delivery.

- Listen to great communicators—not to imitate them but to learn from them. I try to do this on a fairly regular basis. As I listen, I ask myself, "Why is my mind wandering right now?" or "What are they doing that is keeping me engaged with this message?" or "How are they illustrating that particular point?"

> **My overall goal in communicating a message is for both my "head" and my "heart" to come out of my mouth.**

My overall goal in communicating a message is for both my "head" and my "heart" to come out of my mouth. Because I am delivering God's Word, I want to share something for people to think about (head) and something to move them (heart) towards obedience to God. There were certainly times when people told me that my preaching ministry wasn't feeding them, but the closer I got to communicating both "head" and "heart," the less I would hear those kinds of comments.

Preparation Time

I have a friend who has consulted professionally with executives in the oil industry. One day I asked him what distinguished exceptional CEOs from good ones. His answer, from working closely with many of them, had nothing to do with differing skill levels. Instead, the exceptional leaders had developed an intuitive gift, which others had not, for knowing the most important things to do on any given day, and then doing them. In those famous words of Goethe: "Things which matter most must never be at the mercy of things which matter least."[24]

Just like money, time needs to be managed well if we are to leverage its potential. We do that by prioritizing and planning in advance rather than simply reacting to demands as they come at us. Our priorities must ultimately be reduced to those few, most important things that need to be done in a week to fulfill our core mission. For those of us who preach or teach regularly, adequate study, prayer, and reflection time need to be at the top of that short list.

Many pastors with preaching responsibilities find it helpful to plan their weeks in half-day blocks of time, and then primarily do only one type of work in each of those blocks, such as counseling, administration, visitation, leadership development, and, of course, study. Usually half-day blocks are sufficient periods to accommodate interruptions and still engage a task adequately. Doing many different things in a short period of time may be exhilarating, but it usually also keeps us from engaging important things sufficiently.

Message preparation, in particular, requires an uninterrupted block of time. It also deserves those hours in a day when we are the most alert and creative. Some of us are much more creative in the morning hours, others, at night. Unfortunately, some of us are also most efficient, if not creative, when we are pressed by deadlines and feel the adrenaline-pumping pressure to produce. That may be fine, but deadline pressures are generally not an excuse to procrastinate until Saturday night.

This is especially challenging for bi-vocational pastors, but as a full time pastor I found that my week could easily fill up, instead, just counseling people. I eventually began to sense that I was hurting the whole congregation by spending too much time with people one-on-one. I had a heart for individual people, a kind of mercy gift that way, but I also realized that I could either spend hours trying to help one person or invest some of those hours in preparing a message that would help everyone. Paul Lowenberg, my father-in-law, was a great preacher. He would say to me, "I like to think I'm counseling *in* my preaching."

Nothing is more potent than God's Word made alive to people by His Spirit. Influential ministry leaders know this and give their best to it.

CHAPTER 9

Change Management

> *"Be strong and courageous,
> because you will lead these people to inherit the land
> I swore to their ancestors to give them."*
> JOSHUA 1:6

Most of us have a love-hate relationship with change. We love it when it clearly benefits us or when we think everyone else needs to change for our sake. But when change robs us of that secure attachment to the familiar or when it's forced on us against our will, it's an easy thing to resent. I never like it when I go to a restaurant and discover they've changed the menu. Inevitably they've dropped the one thing I always order. Neither do I appreciate when a vendor changes its website. I used to know how to get around the site and order things, but the unfamiliarity of the new site is often confusing, even if it can actually do more than it did before.

No wonder the ability to lead people successfully through seasons of change is an especially sophisticated leadership skill. It's actually more of an art than a science—listening to the direction of the Holy Spirit for new steps and yet bringing as many people along with us as possible, with all of them loving each other in the end. Challenging as that may be, managing change is part of what leadership is all about. Without change people won't grow, ministries won't develop in effectiveness, and problems will be left to fester.

As we will see, it takes a lot of wisdom-guided courage to be a change agent. Courage is one of the most defining characteristics of effective leaders, especially in this area. It struck me one day as a pastor that the church I was serving probably didn't want a pastor who had lots of courage but no wisdom. That would be recklessness. But what good would a pastor be who had wisdom but no courage? Everything would stagnate. Wisdom guides leadership, but courage fuels it.

Because of the challenges inherent in change leadership, let me begin with an overall perspective on the issue followed by a list of some change management ideas.

An Overall Perspective

Because change can be emotionally charged as well as strategically important, managing those emotions in ourselves and others is necessarily part of any change management strategy. Some changes will be easy, but for most people navigating major change will require them to face some anxieties and negative emotions. The unknown can breed anxiety; the unfamiliar can breed discomfort; changes in roles and expectations can breed insecurity; the consequences of growth can breed confusion; feeling inconvenienced can breed anger; taking on new responsibilities can breed fear. If we aren't sensitive to the "anxiety factor" others are experiencing during major change processes, lasting change may be imperiled.

> **We lead in attitude before we lead in behavior.**

As change-leaders this starts with us. We need to learn to manage our own emotions first. The challenge is to be that "non-anxious presence"[25] in the midst of the change-related anxieties that may surround us. We encountered this principle in chapter five when we discussed the need for leaders to be the attitude-setters. We lead in attitude before we lead in behavior.

For change management this means staying sensitive to

people's anxieties while not caving in to them. Leadership steadiness in us creates an atmosphere of reassurance, hope, and stability in the people and ministries around us. But if we panic along with everyone else, the possibility of change is probably doomed. This is where courage comes in. Courage is not the absence of fear; rather, it's not letting our fears dominate us, or others.

Once we've learned to manage our own anxieties, we're in a better position to help others walk through their anxieties. Unfortunately our tendency is to get impatient with people who are distressed over change and judge their feelings instead of validating them. It usually isn't a good day in my marriage when I find myself saying to my wife, "Honey, you shouldn't feel that way." The problem is, she does feel that way, whether she should or not. Instead of respecting her enough to validate that those feelings are real, and going from there, I am judging her feelings, putting her on the defensive, and creating sides in what could become a serious argument.

We need courage to stay non-anxious ourselves, but we also need patience to walk people through their emotions, giving them time to understand and process change. As a pastor, it took me a while to catch on to the fact that new change initiatives in the church would require that I spend much more time than usual simply listening to people one-on-one or in small groups, empathizing with their anxieties, helping them understand the big picture, and assuring them that they were valued no matter what they felt about the changes. The issue is not that we agree with everyone's opinions, but, as in any relationship, validating people's feelings rather than judging them will have a significant impact on how they respond.

We can do better as ministry leaders than simply writing off anyone who doesn't see things the way we do or accusing people of having a rebellious spirit if they don't immediately buy into our vision. Not everyone will walk through change with us, but a lot more will if we treat people respectfully and are patient with the personal and emotional issues the change may surface for them.

With that overarching perspective in place, here are a set of suggestions for walking people through change—anxieties and all.

Change Management Strategies

1. *Avoid change for change's sake.*

Some leaders get bored and change things just to keep themselves engaged, or at least amused. Other leaders are driven by ego issues. Because the previous leader did things a certain way, they feel some sort of inner mandate to do them differently. Yet again, some leaders push for change out of an apparent need for everything around them to conform to their own preferences. None of these are legitimate reasons to change things, and they rarely serve the best interests of the people and ministries around us.

2. *Always emphasize mission over preference.*

Change should always be tied to mission. In healthy ministries, the mission answers the question as to why changes are needed, not the status quo or people's personal preferences or the leader's insecurities. Mission always focuses us upward and outward. Otherwise we become inward. Our convictions about mission should justify change.

> Change should always be tied to mission.

One board member in a strong church I pastored said to me one day, "I don't particularly like the music we've been singing lately, but when I look over during worship and see my son holding my grandson in one arm and lifting his other hand to the Lord, it's worth it." He went on, "What I really want more than my favorite music is a church that my children and grandchildren want to attend." That would be mission over preference.

CHANGE MANAGEMENT

3. *Pace changes wisely and realistically.*

Too much change can ruin good change. Changing everything all at once overwhelms people and often does more long-term damage than not changing things at all. Good ministry leaders are often quite creative, but it's hard to follow a leader who comes up with a new directional idea every day or a new vision for the church every few months. There is value in developing good systems for reaching and growing people, and then working those systems over and over again. Changing the systems too often can keep them from ever taking root in the ministry culture and becoming effective.

4. *Assess the real reasons for resistance to change.*

It may be the condition of people's hearts—spiritual coldness, complacency, self-serving agendas. Or the problem could lie with us as leaders. Perhaps people sense that we expect more of them than we do of ourselves, or they no longer trust us for some reason. More often than not, however, people resist change because the process for bringing about change is flawed. If the way that change is pushed forward feels manipulative, hasty, or groundless, people's first instinct will be to protect themselves from it. Even good change, brought about in the wrong way, can feel bad.

5. *Create a sense of urgency.*

People will change either because they want to or because they have to. They can want to change if they see a compelling vision of what the future could look like. That future always needs to be connected to something they value, such as seeing people reached

> **People will change either because they want to or because they have to.**

with the gospel and lives changed. But sometimes bad news, even a crisis, is necessary for people to change. This is sometimes referred to as "building a burning platform."[26] It motivates people to jump.

During an economic downturn that adversely affected the church I was pastoring, I wanted to hide the church's financial problems from the members. But there was no change in giving until I risked bringing the hard realities to light so that people could feel the urgency and take ownership of doing something about it. Urgency can be a powerful motivator. The caution, however, is to avoid making everything a crisis, all of the time. People will start feeling manipulated and will tune out.

6. *Never underestimate the importance of process.*

In spite of our desire to just "make things happen," ignoring processes that help other people adapt to and feel a part of the change usually comes with a high price tag. Sometimes three extra months, or even an extra year, of preparing people for change can accomplish more in the long run than pushing change through in a hurry.

I once pushed through a church-wide, small-group ministry before the congregation was ready. Most people felt no ownership of the program, and it fizzled. As tempting as it is to shortcut the process, and as impatient as we can be as leaders with the time that process takes, if people aren't on board with us we won't accomplish anything anyway. Keep the process as efficient as possible, but don't neglect it or take it for granted.

7. *Build a team of influencers to champion the change.*

It's difficult, if not impossible, for a leader to change an entire ministry culture alone. We need to look at the ministries we lead and ask, "Who are the people who have the most influence with others?" If they have been envisioned with the benefits of the change, they'll become champions of it. And their opinions carry weight.

Before major decisions on my church boards, for instance, I would meet personally with a few key board members and prepare them for the discussion. By sharing with them ahead of time what was in my heart and giving them time to ask questions and process, their buy-in and influence became my ally in the larger group. On the other hand, if the people with influence showed up at the meeting unprepared and opposed to the change, it would have little chance of being implemented.

8. *Build ownership by letting people participate in the planning.*

When we walk people through change, our goal isn't for them to reluctantly submit out of respect for our authority but to be enthusiastically committed to the change. That doesn't happen by telling people what they should do, but by bringing people into the process early to solicit their feedback and help. People will feel enthusiasm and ownership for what they help to create. As a leader, I could often predict what the outcomes would probably be, but I would involve key leaders and volunteers in the dreaming and planning process anyway. Having people feel ownership was too important not to let people help shape the change with me.

9. *Bring the affected parties into the loop ahead of time.*

Few things are more disheartening than to find out that someone has made a decision that affects us without first consulting with us. It feels uncaring and disrespectful. If people are going to be affected by change, let them know before the final decision is made. Perhaps a service time is going to change, or a ministry is going to stop, or a group's leader is going to change. All of these things affect people. If possible, consult with them ahead of time and ask for their feedback. Good change will hopefully bring about many wins, but there may also be some losses. Be honest with people about what they will lose as well as what they will gain as change takes place.

10. *Don't demonize the opponents to change.*

Their disagreement may not necessarily mean disloyalty. Sometimes leaders get frustrated and develop unhealthy habits of burning relational bridges with people who disagree with them. Yet it's amazing how, with time, people will come around to a point of view if we stay steady but sweet.

To help minimize opposition, try to not take things of value away from people as change is implemented. Instead, phase in new behaviors and ministries while keeping old ones intact for a while, if resources allow. Eventually, the fruitful will overtake the unfruitful. It's important that people don't feel like what they love has been taken away from them without something of compensating value given back. Adding value to people as opposed to subtracting value is the currency of human relationships.

11. *Remember that behaviors change faster than personalities.*

Every ministry organization has a personality as well as a set of behaviors or activities. The personality is sometimes referred to as the culture of the organization. Changing a ministry's culture is usually a long process, but behaviors are easier to change and are therefore usually the best starting points for bringing change. As long as wrong behaviors are not being rewarded, the culture will eventually begin to change as well.

When I assumed one particular pastorate, it became clear to me that the people felt strongly that certain program issues needed to be addressed and fixed. Doing so created some fairly quick congregational wins that we could celebrate and use to energize further steps forward. Start by changing behaviors that everyone knows need to change.

12. *Never forget the power of trust.*

In his book *The Speed of Trust* Stephen Covey identifies trust as the "one thing which, if removed will destroy the most powerful government, the most successful business, the most thriving economy, the most influential leadership" and yet if embraced can create "unparalleled success and prosperity in every dimension of life."[27] Trust is the foundation of our relationship with Christ and the essential ingredient in any healthy human relationship. It is also the one non-negotiable for leading a group of people through change.

Trust, in many ways, ties together everything we've been discussing regarding change management. If people don't trust us, we probably won't lead them very far. I once led a congregation through a change of service times on Sunday morning. To be honest, I cut some corners and made the decision with only a small group of leaders without processing it with the congregation beforehand. I broke the rules and simply announced one Sunday that we were going to change.

Because it affected so many people without their input, there should have been at least a minor revolt, but there was nothing but goodwill. Why? Because, in that case, the change was tied to our mission and I had been there long enough as their pastor that trust carried the day. I'm not saying that being trusted as a leader is an excuse for bypassing process or ignoring people's feedback, but trust does broaden our influence and enable us to lead in remarkably effective and efficient ways.

Trust is more than a feeling. It isn't something ethereal. Neither is it anything that we're entitled to. It's confidence that's earned through character and faithfulness and consistently looking out for the best interests of the people we serve. When it comes to change management, the real leadership question isn't, "What around me needs to change?" but "What in me needs to change so I become a leader people trust?"

SECTION 4

Stamina and Stability

Understanding the difference between self-denial and self-neglect can be a freeing realization.

- Self-denial is the willful setting aside of a legitimate need for a higher purpose. Self-neglect is a violation of our stewardship.
- Self-denial has everything to do with sacrifice, discipline, and love. Self-neglect has all of the trademarks of irresponsibility, lack of discipline, and inattentiveness.
- Self-denial is what it takes to follow Jesus. Self-neglect is the road to putting ourselves at risk physically, emotionally, and spiritually.
- Self-denial will make us stronger, but self-neglect will leave us weaker. The difference is in the fruit.

Unfortunately, we can experience a sense of false guilt when we care for ourselves in physical and emotional ways. Guilt is like cholesterol—there is the good kind and the bad kind. The bad kind makes us feel guilty whenever we take a day off, read a book that isn't about ministry, work at a hobby, or do enjoyable things that refill our emotional tanks. Bad guilt makes self-neglect easy.

On top of that is the assault of the Enemy simply because being a leader has put a target on our backs. We must not neglect the demands of that battle either. It's important that we prevail.

Leadership is a wonderful calling even though there are moments when it can be draining and frustrating. By defying self-neglect and developing stamina in our lives we can stay in the fight until our work is done.

CHAPTER 10

Physical Health

"Do you not know that your bodies are temples of the Holy Spirit . . . ?"
1 Corinthians 6:19

During my twenties it was easy to think that good health was sort of a birthright. My metabolism kept me skinny no matter what I ate and my energy levels stayed high no matter how hard I pushed myself. I ran for exercise, but not nearly as much as I had to thirty years later in order to stay in shape. Back then it was all too tempting to ignore my body and take my health for granted as I went all out for Jesus.

With time, however, it wasn't only *chronology* that caught with me but *theology*. Although Paul rightly taught that spiritual health is of more lasting value than physical health (1 Tim. 4:8), that didn't stop him from confronting the excessively low view of the physical body that ran rampant through Greek dualistic philosophy. "Your bodies," he said, "are temples of the Holy Spirit." Furthermore, "You were bought at a price. Therefore honor God with your bodies" (1 Cor. 6:19-20).

Christianity has always held to a high view of the human body. Christ lays claim to our bodies. He redeemed them at the price of His shed blood, and He has an eternal plan for them—resurrection. Our bodies are also a "sanctuary"—they give residence to the Holy Spirit's indwelling presence. This implies not only a call to sexual purity but a call to steward our bodies in a holistic lifestyle of worship and service.

Practical concerns regarding our physical stamina and survivability are at stake here as well. Ministry is obviously more a marathon than a sprint, and our bodies are hard-wired into that run. Low energy, lethargic attitudes, emotional instability, and sickness can interrupt that run, or even end it prematurely. We may choose to ignore the symptoms or write them off as little more than spiritual warfare, but more often than not they are signs of serious wear and tear on our bodies.

All of this makes caring for our physical health important. Unfortunately, many of us in ministry leadership aren't doing well at it. Bob Wells of Duke Divinity School put it rather succinctly: "North American churches have in common not only the cross and a love of Christ, but also a pastorate whose health is fast becoming cause for concern."[28]

So where do we start? Here are three areas that, if given the right kind of attention, will contribute significantly to our physical health: (1) rest, (2) diet, and (3) exercise.

Rest

Pastor, professor, and best-selling author, Barbara Brown Taylor, has some rather frank things to say about the refusal to rest. "I do not mean to make an idol of health, but it does seem to me that at least some of us have made an idol of exhaustion. The only time we know we have done enough is when we are running on empty and when the ones we love most are the ones we see the least. When we lie down to sleep at night, we offer our full appointment calendars to God in lieu of prayer, believing that God—who is as busy as we are—will surely understand."[29]

Rest isn't an easy issue for many of us in leadership, especially those of us who've been raised with a strong work ethic. We either tend to feel guilty about doing things for ourselves when we rest, or we stay so consumed with the demands of work and the needs of people that we never rest. There's also that seemingly relentless gap between the way things ideally could be and the way they actually are, making it even harder for us to slow down. But in the process we end up exhausting our bodies and depleting our physical reserves.

There's a spiritual dimension to rest that we tend to overlook. Jesus once told the leaders-in-training around Him, "My yoke is easy and my burden is light" (Matt. 11:30). For many of us, the act of resting is a step of faith—daring to trust that we are, indeed, yoked to Christ; that things will be fine without us, at least for a while. Rest in that sense is actually a crucifying work that humbles our egos and puts to death our sense of indispensability, making us lean more fully on God.

> My simple rule of thumb is to sleep nightly, stop weekly, and escape annually.

Neither should rest be mistaken for laziness. Being a truly good leader takes a lot of hard work, making it extra challenging to find a healthy work-life balance. But it can be done if we have a plan. What I am *not* advocating is being careless with our leadership responsibilities or allowing personal distractions to pull us away from work too many times. Laziness militates against true rest; hard work complements it.

What it takes to work hard and rest well is *rhythm*. My simple rule of thumb is to *sleep nightly, stop weekly,* and *escape annually*.

I mention sleep first because an alarming number of people in our culture (and in the ministry) are living with sleep deprivation. Lack of sleep dulls our thinking, slows our response times, makes us fragile emotionally, and depletes our resistance to sickness. Sometimes getting a good night's sleep is the best thing we can do for ourselves.

For stopping weekly, the cycle of one day in seven is a biblical, healthy, and achievable rhythm. The principle to break from regular work one day in seven is, in fact, a cycle that God embedded in the created order all the way back in Genesis 1.

Sabbath is God's plan to restore us mentally, emotionally, and physically. In the Old Testament the weekly Sabbath was Friday sundown to Saturday sundown. A pastor's weekly day off should obviously not be Sunday, and often Saturday is not realistic either. Many ministry leaders take Mondays off, some Thursdays or another day of the week. I personally took Fridays off so that I could go into the weekend more rested.

The day of the week we choose for rest is not as important as having adequate time to redirect and reflect; to do things that are unlike work, and to live at a slower pace. Physical activities, including working with our hands, can be a good alternative to the rather sedentary nature of what we as ministry leaders do the rest of the week. Resting may also include relational time with family, spending non-ministry time with the Lord, reading books, working on hobbies, or engaging in any number of personal activities other than taking ministry-related phone calls or answering emails from work. Some of us are too addicted to our Smartphones and hand-held devices.

On an annual basis, it's important to break away from work long enough to more fully escape the constant demands of ministry leadership. Part of rest is physically changing the pace of life. The other is getting away from our work mentally and emotionally, which also serves to restore us physically. The kind of recovery that both our bodies and our souls need takes time. In that sense, a single two-week vacation can do more for us than a series of two- or three-day breaks throughout the year.

Diet

What we eat affects how we feel, what we look like, and the energy we have to engage God's calling on our lives. While regular rest is a base-line activity for the care of our bodies, we can't overlook proper nutrition when it comes to our personal health and overall well-being.

Unfortunately, obesity has grown into a major global epidemic over the past several decades. In the United States, more than two-thirds of adults are now overweight and one-third are obese. Mayo Clinic reports: "Although there are genetic and hormonal influences on body weight, obesity occurs when a person takes in more calories than they are able to burn through exercise and normal daily activities. The body stores these excess calories as fat."[30] Obesity, in turn, brings with it the risk of heart disease, diabetes, and high blood pressure, to name just a few health-related problems.

A Baylor University research study revealed that "more than a third of American clergy members are obese, with stress, longer hours, being underpaid, and lack of self-care among the reasons."[31] On the other hand, this same study indicated that the prevention of obesity was clearly correlated to clergy who took a day off each week, had a sabbatical, and were a part of a peer support group. We've discussed rest as an essential key to taking care of our bodies. What we must not miss, however, is how interrelated rest is to eating habits and physical obesity. Stress is often the link.[32]

A practical approach to diet was also included in the Baylor research project. It suggested: fasting from junk food; eating less meat; paying attention to our hunger so as not to eat more than necessary to satisfy it; taking care not to waste food; and never eating without saying thanks as a way of reminding us that food is God's gift.[33] These are all small but important practices that can make tangible differences, both to our weight and our well-being.

> **Maintaining a healthy diet doesn't need to be complicated.**

Many educational resources on good nutrition are readily available from doctors, reputable websites, and book stores. Crash dieting often has only short term benefits. The best advice, if possible, is to develop lifelong eating habits that control weight and boost energy, as opposed to binge dieting all the time. Maintaining a healthy diet doesn't need to be complicated. The key is to moderate our intake of sweets, high starch foods, and "bad" fats (as opposed to "healthy" fats)—and be careful of those second helpings of food at the dinner table when we're already fairly full.

As with rest, there's also a spiritual dimension to eating. All of us eat for survival, most of us eat for enjoyment, and many of us eat for the experience of community. But sometimes we eat to fill emotional and spiritual holes in our lives. We misuse food to cope with stress, indulge our sensuality, or resolve otherwise unresolved identity issues. Yet as followers of Christ we have been made new in Him. Jesus is our healing portion and our sustaining strength. "Therefore, if anyone is in Christ, the new creation has come: The old has gone, the new is here!" (2 Cor. 5:17). In Him we can overcome habits of over-eating, under-eating, and wrong eating. We *can* be free to live rightly, and even eat rightly, through new life in Him.

Exercise

In general, many of us could afford to eat less and move more. It's a common misconception that exercise alone will solve our problems—or diet alone for that matter. The combination of the two, along with adequate rest, is the best prescription for taking good care of our bodies.

As with diet, just the thought of regular exercise overwhelms most us with guilt. Medical professionals claim that we should get a minimum of thirty minutes of physical exercise every day.[34] That can feel pretty out of reach for most of us. Fortunately, the benefits of physical activity throughout a day are cumulative, so it doesn't necessarily need to be thirty continuous minutes of exercise.

Walking is a good starting place. If we go from doing nothing to taking a brisk walk every day, the benefits health-wise can actually be quite remarkable. Walking is also a good multi-tasking exercise. We can both walk and fellowship with the Lord, or build a relationship with a friend, or think about a leadership decision. Walking also stimulates the flow of blood to our brains and helps us think more clearly.[35]

Of course there are many other ways we can stay physically active throughout the day as well. Playing with our kids, taking the stairs instead of an elevator, cleaning the garage—all of these exerting activities contribute to the cumulative benefits of physical exercise.

For those who are physically able, the best regimen for more vigorous exercise is a combination of cardiovascular workouts, resistance training, and stretching.[36] Cardiovascular exercise helps with circulation, heart health, energy level, and cholesterol reduction. Boosting muscle mass through resistance workouts, like lifting weights, can increase our metabolism and actually cause our bodies to burn fat even when we aren't working out. As we age, stretching exercises also become increasingly important for maintaining flexibility.

All of this takes time, unfortunately, and some discipline. We need to decide that this is important. Start with small goals and build up to bigger ones. Exercise with someone for the accountability and the joy of it. While celebrating successes, however, we should avoid always using food to reward ourselves. We should also make exercise a part of our weekly schedule, doing some exercise several times a week as opposed to a lot of it sporadically.

Staying motivated long-term is a big challenge for many of us. But when I'm exercising I often remind myself that I'm doing this for a family that needs me and for a church that wants its pastor to be around for a while. The same goes for eating and resting. Because of our roles as family members and ministry leaders, a lot of people are counting on us. As I once heard someone put it, "If we can't do this for ourselves, let's at least do it for the sake of those who love us."

Above all, let us rest and eat and exercise for the glory of God. He created these bodies of ours, and He owns them. We are stewards of the health and energy He has given us. They are gifts from His hand, yet they include boundaries that we must respect. Let's not push our bodies to the breaking point or eat ourselves to an early grave or erode our stamina through self-neglect and lack of discipline.

The apostle Paul put it right, *"Honor God with your body."* May our response be, "Yes, Lord" and "help us, Lord" and "to your glory we will do it, Lord."

CHAPTER 11

Emotional Resilience

"We are hard pressed on every side, but not crushed; perplexed, but not in despair."
2 Corinthians 4:8

As he waited final word certifying his election as the first president of the United States, George Washington lamented to a colleague that his "movements to the chair of government will be accompanied with feelings not unlike those of a culprit who is going to the place of his execution."[37] As morbid as that may sound, Washington was probably on to something. Leading the general public isn't easy. Up until then he had been a highly acclaimed military hero, but all that was about to end.

Leadership usually means getting hurt at some point, in some way. One of my executive pastors, Chip Johnson, helped me with this. He had an intuitive brilliance about him when it came to leadership systems, and he accurately read my discouragement one day. Borrowing from a baseball metaphor he said, "Jim, people will cheer you on when you hit a home run, and those same people will boo you down when you strike out, but not many of them are willing to step up to the plate themselves."

Our ministry skills may be impressive, but without the inner fortitude to step up to the plate or the emotional ability to cope with the risks and criticisms that come with it, we probably won't be able to lead. Leadership takes both *missional courage* and *emotional capacity*. The two are inseparable. They are what set truly effective leaders apart from the others. But the emotional dimension is often overlooked in leadership.

Highly successful pastor of Willow Creek Community Church, Bill Hybels, wrote an article in *Leadership Journal* several years ago entitled "Watching Your Gauges." In it he confessed, "The spiritual and physical aspects of life were important, but I had failed to consider another area essential to healthy ministry—emotional strength. I was so emotionally depleted I couldn't even discern the activity or the call of God on my life."[38]

Emotional depletion goes by many names—burnout, exhaustion, stress overload, discouragement, depression, nervous breakdown, instability, or even crisis of faith. Every leader is vulnerable. Building healthy emotional capacity, or emotional resilience, is crucial to handling and outliving the stressors that leadership subjects us to. Because we're interconnected beings, taking care of ourselves spiritually and physically is certainly important, but we need to be honest and give attention to our emotional lives as well.

In his groundbreaking book, *Margin*, Dr. Richard Swenson, MD, underscores this by first explaining: "Margin is the amount allowed beyond that which is needed. It is something held in reserve for contingencies or unanticipated situations."[39] He then goes on to suggest that, "Of the four margins—emotional energy, physical energy, time, and finances—margin in emotional energy is paramount. When we are emotionally resilient, we can confront our problems with a sense of hope and power. . . . Emotional overload saps our strength, paralyzes our resolve, and maximizes our vulnerability, leaving the door open for even further margin erosion."[40]

Given the importance of developing emotional resilience, how do we do so without, at the same time, becoming callous and disconnecting ourselves emotionally from the people we love and the ministries we lead?

Our Thinking Patterns

Emotional management starts with how we think. Feelings are not causes, they are effects; they are the result of what we tell

> **Feelings are not causes, they are effects; they are the result of what we tell ourselves.**

ourselves. Sometimes we tell ourselves true things, other times not. What we tell ourselves, however, right or wrong, will affect our ability to cope emotionally with what we perceive to be reality around us. It's no wonder that Paul, in the verse immediately preceding his declaration, "and the peace of God will be with you" (Phil. 4:9), tells us to guard our thoughts.

Here are four misbeliefs or wrong ways of thinking that I've found to be common among leaders. Each one of them depletes emotional reserves.

Performance-Driven Thinking

Performance-driven thinking centers on the misbelief, "I am what I do." But if I'm defined by what I do, who will I be and how will I feel about myself when I can no longer 'do'? If I fail, or if I'm passed over for a position, or if I need to retire, performance-driven thinking will set me up for an identity crisis. Building emotional resilience starts with refusing to wrap too much of our identity into what we do.

Untamed, performance-driven thinking can also build an unhealthy drivenness into the motivational structure of our lives. Chronic drivenness, though it may appear noble, is usually more about us than about God's calling. Because we believe that we are what we do, we "need to be needed" too much and take leadership conflicts far too personally. At the same time, our ability to deal with discouragement is seriously diminished, all because identity-related performance issues are driving us at our core.

Performance-driven thinking can also infect our relationship with God. I appreciate the honesty with which ministry director and author Fil Anderson describes his own slide into emotional burnout: "As I threw myself into my new ministry, I once again lost the ability to distinguish between my work and myself. . . . My default nature is set to believe that God's acceptance, love, and care for me is directly proportional to my level of activity for God. This belief system—the more I do for God, the more God will love me—has dictated my every waking activity more than anything else. *And it has threatened to starve my soul*"[41] (emphasis mine).

Perfection-Based Thinking

If performance-driven thinking says, "I am what I do," then perfection-based thinking says, "What I do, I must do perfectly." My wife is a self-confessed, recovering perfectionist. She had to die to a lot of that when she married me, of course! But I've often heard her describe how perfectionism made her look at life in all-or-nothing terms. Things were either all bad or all good, nothing in between; either a 1 or a 10, but never a 5; either 100 percent in, or not involved at all. Perfectionistic thinking is also shot through with too many unrealistic oughts and shoulds—"I *should* never make a mistake." "I always *ought* to have the answer."

> Perfection-based thinking also keeps us trapped in a kind of false shame.

Or, worse yet, "People *should* be what I want them to be, *perfect.*"

In her insightful article, "Good Enough!" counselor and writer Paula Rinehart describes her own battle with performance and perfectionistic tendencies. One day, at the point of exhaustion, she found herself asking her husband, "Why do you suppose that God makes it so hard to serve Him?" No matter where she looked, she felt like she was never measuring up. But a major turning point came when, in her words, "I finally realized that my 'inner critic' was not the voice of God."[42] It's one thing to obey the Lord, to do the best we can and leave it at that; it's quite another to never escape those three haunting words, "not good enough."

Perfection-based thinking also keeps us trapped in a kind

of false shame. Because we perceive ourselves as always falling short, we not only feel guilty, we feel worthless. Shame equates our lack of perfection with a lack of personal worth and makes us hide. This only deepens the lies. Emotional health is not possible without truthfully and honestly facing who we are and what we are feeling.

Although I'm not an all-out perfectionist, I still had to work through issues of guilt versus shame in my life, between knowing I'm imperfect on one hand and feeling worthless on the other. It's here that we need the gospel. In Christ, our worth is not based on *our* perfection but on *His*. The gospel frees us from *self-*righteousness and gives us a brand new starting point in Jesus for true honesty, freedom, and emotional healing of every kind.

People-Pleasing Thinking

This is a challenge for most leaders I know, and I'm as susceptible as anyone. But the apostle Paul leaves us no room for compromise. "If I were still trying to please people, I would not be a servant of Christ" (Gal. 1:10). Obviously, part of the problem is a spiritual one. We fear people more than we fear God.

However, some of our people-pleasing tendencies are actually the shadow side of our otherwise good leadership intentions. We want to be sensitive to people, care for them, and influence them to follow our lead as we follow Christ. And they will probably not follow us if they don't like us. But when taken too far, we can cross a dangerous line into unhealthy dependence on people's approval.

Nowhere does this become more poignant than when we are criticized. The emotional consequence can be devastating if we don't handle our critics and their criticisms properly. Here are a few guidelines I've learned over the years to help manage the pain of not pleasing everyone:

- **Stay a learner.** There is often at least a shred of truth to the criticisms we receive, even if most of it is unfair.

- ☐ **Avoid personalizing the criticism.** We need to stay humble enough to not take personal offense at having been criticized, leading to over-reactions and misunderstandings of the real issues on our part.

- ☐ **Factor in their pain.** Unfortunately, people who are hurting tend to hurt others. Some criticism is little more than people projecting their internal conflicts on us.

- ☐ **Ask trusted people.** When we're hurt by criticism we tend to lose objectivity, so it's good to have spouses, friends, and mentoring leaders who can help us sort through what's valid, what isn't, and how to best respond.

- ☐ **Pray.** Our critics need prayer for their issues, and we need the Holy Spirit's help to heal our own hurt.

Problem-Centered Thinking

Our emotional reserves can also be seriously depleted by worrying too much. As ministry leaders, problems confront us everywhere we look—personal problems, relational problems, financial problems, organizational problems—the list seems endless. To make things worse, some of us have temperaments that lean more towards melancholic pessimism than joyful optimism. It's hard to cope with life emotionally, let alone navigate the challenges of leadership, when we feel burdened down all the time.

A young ministry leader who had gone through a lot of discouraging times told me that one day he and his wife made the decision that they were not just going to *survive*, but they were going to *thrive*. They decided to become people of faith, to live with joy and not let their problems determine their perspective. He described to me the incredible turnaround that occurred in their attitudes and their enjoyment of life. It was later that some wonderful breakthroughs took place in the ministry they led as well.

> **Our focus can be on the greatness of God, not the greatness of our problems.**

The apostle Paul counseled, "Do not be anxious about anything" (Phil. 4:6). Thriving in spite of our problems is part of our privilege as Spirit-anointed, God-called leaders. "With God all things are possible," Jesus said (Matt. 19:26). Our focus can be on the greatness of God, not the greatness of our problems. Prayer can be more than an exercise in worry. We are people of faith, and faith believes "that he exists and that he rewards those who earnestly seek him" (Heb. 11:6).

Our Lifestyle Choices

It's difficult for many of us in leadership to be honest about our emotional struggles. But honesty with ourselves and with others can begin a journey to both spiritual and emotional renewal. Along the way there will be not only new ways of thinking but lifestyle choices that can enhance emotional health. Here are a few:

Take Time for Yourself

In spite of the false guilt that may accompany it, we must never underestimate our need to periodically relax, laugh, have fun, engage activities that renew us emotionally, and, in general, "unstring the bow" of our ministry lives. Writer George Grant crafts a powerful word picture to explain this:

> At the end of the thirteenth century when the Norman English bowmen began to pioneer the powerful new military technology of the long bow ... they discovered that the very best precaution that a bowman could take for his weapon was simply to unstring the bow when it was not in use. To release the tension, relax the pressure,

and relieve the strain allowed the bow to last longer, snap back faster, and set arrows to flight further. A bow that was never unstrung would quickly lose its effectiveness. A bow that was never relaxed became useless as an offensive weapon.[43]

Let Go of Offenses

I was once really hurt by someone who attended the church I pastored. He would take me out for coffee, criticize me for an hour or two, and then let me pay. I began to second-guess my calling into ministry. Then he disappeared for a couple of years, only to return a broken person. He reached out to me again, but this time because he needed a pastor. He never asked me for forgiveness, but I knew I had a decision to make. Would my future be encumbered with offenses I refused to let go of, or would I give him the second chance that Christ has given every one of us and walk away free?

By God's grace, I let it go. Forgiveness unclogs us spiritually and frees us from living as the victims of other people's behaviors. Carrying around emotional baggage is exhausting. If we're to have the emotional reserves we need for the really important things, we must forgive people and move on.

Work Within Your Gifting

Although servant leadership may require us to do whatever needs to be done at any given time, over the long run our primary responsibilities need to align with what we are gifted to do. It takes hard work to do anything well, but when we constantly endeavor to do things outside of our gifting, the emotional toll can become overwhelming.

Sometimes we compensate by over-delegating our core responsibilities to other team members, but that is a functionally poor way to lead and will likely backfire, leading to even more stress. Ultimately, we need the Lord to help us position our primary responsibilities around those areas where we are most gifted—whether it be teaching, leading, administrating, mentoring, or care-giving.

Change What You Can—Avoid Trying to Control What You Can't

In his classic book *Stress/Unstress*, Dr. Keith Sehnert describes research studies that show control issues to be at the heart of stress management.[44] The more we feel in control, the less stress we tend to experience. The less we feel in control of the decisions we need to make, the more stress we will likely experience. Rush hour traffic would be a good illustration of that.

Unfortunately, ministry leadership is full of variables that we have little control over. At the top of that list would be people. We can influence people, but we can't control them. To try to do so is a recipe for emotional burnout. Margaret Marcuson, in *Leaders Who Last*, advises: "Here is the heart of what it takes to sustain leadership. We move from the impossible—controlling others—to the merely difficult—managing ourselves. When I hear leaders begin with a question like, 'How can I get them to . . . ?' then I know that different questions need to be asked: 'What is my part in the problem? How can I clarify what I think about this issue?'"[45]

Managing ourselves means changing what we can—our schedules, the way we prepare and pre-plan, the priorities we focus on, and the leadership roles we are called to fill. The rest is in God's hands, and we can trust Him to do his part without a lot of stress on ours.

Have a Safe Perspective-Giving Peer Group

Isolation starves us emotionally. And when we *are* with people, some drain us more than others. We need to guard against being alone too much and balance the draining people in our lives with those who encourage us and carry the load with us. It isn't selfish to have health-giving relationships.

Often we hear people say it's lonely at the top, but perhaps we've made leadership lonelier than it needs to be. Even if we're physically isolated from a peer group of other leaders, communication technology and social media are quickly removing our excuses for not staying connected. Emotional health requires that we walk with people who can handle our honesty, understand what we face, know how to pray for us, and stay unthreatened by our success.

CHAPTER 12

Spiritual Prevailing

"If you falter in a time of trouble, how small is your strength!"
Proverbs 24:10

Our spiritual Enemy is real. We're in a war, and we can't take spiritual opposition for granted. I'm convinced that if we are pushing the frontiers of leadership to advance Christ's kingdom, we don't need to look for demons—they will be looking for us. We don't glorify what the Enemy does, but at the same time we acknowledge that we are in a battle and we must learn to prevail in Jesus' name, the One who has defeated Satan through His death on a cross and resurrection from the dead.

Spiritual warfare is an inescapable reality of ministry leadership. When ministries I led began to move forward in effectiveness, invariably we experienced increased spiritual opposition. At one time, I pastored a church in a city where there was a lot of spiritual darkness. So much so that sometimes I had to push myself just to get normal things done in a day. I've occasionally heard missionaries talk about similar kinds of experiences. At other churches I noticed that whenever we came under spiritual attack, the people on my leadership teams started to feel edgy and conflicted with each other. Everything felt annoying, like sandpaper was grating on our spirits. Sometimes

I saw the Enemy come against my wife and daughters with discouragement and hurtful experiences.

Paul's concern at the end of his letter to the Ephesians is the same daunting issue that faces all of us as ministry leaders: our capacity to "be strong in the Lord and in his mighty power" in order to "stand against the devil's schemes" (Eph. 6:10–11). Paul here reminds us that our real enemy is not people who aggravate us, critics who oppose us, or even persecutors who kill us. Our real war is transacted in unseen spiritual realms against sinister forces, "against the powers of this dark world and against the spiritual forces of evil in the heavenly realms" (Eph. 6:12).

Wars such as these are not won through conflict resolution or strategic planning alone. As helpful as those activities are, they don't engage the power structures resident in spiritual realms. Taken alone, they're about as effective as attacking armored tanks with water pistols. So Paul exhorted the Ephesians to "put on the full armor of God, so that when the day of evil comes, you may be able to stand your ground" (v. 13).

He then linked each piece of armor to essential gospel realities such as salvation, truth, righteousness, faith, Word, and readiness (vv. 14–17). These pieces of armor function through the power of the Holy Spirit and, taken together, this "armor of God" proves spiritually potent—both offensively and defensively.

Paul then combined the "putting on" of spiritual armor into an "all occasions" assignment: "And pray in the Spirit on all occasions with all kinds of prayers and requests" (v.18). What harnesses the spiritual potency of each piece of spiritual armor? What ties those pieces together into a potent, unified, wearable whole? What foundational activity is common to every victory in the unseen realms? It is prayer—"in the Spirit," of "all kinds," and directed toward "all the Lord's people."

> **One of the great mysteries of the relationship between Christ and His church is that He involves us in His purposes.**

SPIRITUAL PREVAILING

Samuel Chadwick rightfully claimed, "The one concern of the devil is to keep Christians from praying. He fears nothing from prayerless studies, prayerless work and prayerless religion. He laughs at our toil, mocks at our wisdom, but trembles when we pray."[46]

One of the great mysteries of the relationship between Christ and His church is that He involves us in His purposes. He has chosen to work through us rather than around us. This is how we understand prayer. The release of His power comes as we partner with Him, based on His will, in prayer and intercession. Beyond simply nourishing our own spiritual health, prayer is what advances ministry by first engaging spiritual dimensions.

A. C. Dixon, pastor of Spurgeon's Tabernacle, once observed that, "When we rely on organization, we get what organization can do; when we rely on education, we get what education can do; when we rely on eloquence, we get what eloquence can do. But when we rely on prayer, we get what God can do."[47]

It is ultimately "what God can do" that gives us any hope of standing our ground in the spiritual battle around us and against us. Paul's Ephesians 6:18 assertion is that we *can* prevail if our circumstances, experiences, conflicts, and struggles are all bathed in ongoing, saturating praying—*"on all occasions . . . for all the Lord's people."*

> **Intercessors understand that spiritual conflict demands a prayerful fight.**

Intercessory Prayer

Paul here is calling us to *intercessory* prayer. This is praying that is engaged "in the Spirit" but focused on the needs of other people. Intercession is taking up faith-filled prayer on behalf of others, as if calling out to God in their stead. Remarkably, God actually postures Himself to respond to this proxy praying. Intercession paves the way for God's intervention in people's lives and in the circumstances we face. Interceding for others is one of the ways we lead spiritually.

Intercessors understand that spiritual conflict demands a prayerful fight. Intercessory prayer is the act of yearning for God's intervention and calling forth His life-giving power in the places where the Enemy has brought destruction and loss. So Paul calls us to "pray in the Spirit on all occasions . . . for all the Lord's people" (v. 18).

Misconceptions About Intercessors

Unfortunately, stereotypes and misconceptions abound when it comes to intercessory people. Those who do intercede a lot in the Spirit are often branded as emotional, mystical, or unstable. They can seem like spiritual oddities in a world full of naturally normal Christians. So we tend to label and compartmentalize them, all the while exempting ourselves as leaders from a deeper life in prayer and lowering the defenses against the Enemy that we may need more than we realize.

It's also a misconception that intercessors always feel like praying, or at least find it easy. It's true that the more we pray, the more we will want to pray, and the less we pray, the less we will want to. It's also true that there are times when God imparts an unusual urgency and ability to pray in very travailing, connecting ways.

But the act of praying *"for all the Lord's people"* is also a command, making it a choice to be made, even though it isn't always easy. Because prayer brings us into the arena of spiritual conflict, it's common to experience resistance, fatigue, and even discouragement as we try to pray. True intercession may take its toll on us physically and emotionally, even though it strengthens us spiritually.

Obviously, it's the *decision* to pray that is crucial, not the *feeling*. Neither is it hypocritical to pray even when we don't feel like it. God hears our prayer regardless of our emotional condition. He is faithful even when we feel weary or unengaged. He is not weakened by what weakens us. He does not change! The issue isn't how we feel, but what His Spirit can do to engender in us faith and hunger for Him as we simply and willingly give ourselves to intercessory prayer.

Guidelines for Intercession

So how can we who lead others also grow in interceding for others? Here is a short-list of things that I have found personally helpful.

Give God Time

More than anything else, God needs us to give Him time—time to be before Him and time enough for Him to give us His heart. On many occasions I have begun times of prayer not feeling particularly spiritual or motivated. Rather than crumpling under a lot of pressure or false guilt, I would simply begin praying in tongues, letting the Spirit pray through me. Or I would take Scripture and begin praying it back to God. Or I would deliberately start to pray for known, specific needs. With time, God's heart would take hold of my otherwise cold heart. It sometimes felt like I began by praying "in the flesh" only to end up praying "in the Spirit." But it takes time. Start small and let it grow from there. Time with God bends our hearts to His, yielding an inevitable desire to spend even more time with Him.

Stand on the Merits of Christ's Blood Alone

Often at the heart of our spiritual insecurity is self-condemnation, which afflicts us with a debilitating sense of unworthiness. Some people find that this feeling becomes more pronounced as they move deeper into effective intercession. It's part of the spiritual warfare and totally contrary to the gospel. I have frequently had to assert by faith, in spite of my feelings, that my standing before God is based solely on Christ's shed blood not on my impressiveness or self-righteousness. In Christ (not in ourselves), "we may approach God with freedom and confidence" (Eph. 3:12).

Focus on the Spirit's Help

A friend of mine once described his journey into intercession this way: "I used to start praying by first looking inside myself for the desire and strength to pray. It only pulled me down. But I decided to start my times of prayer by looking upward instead of inward, asking the Holy Spirit to come and teach me to pray. It changed everything." The Holy Spirit can, indeed, teach us to pray, and we have the privilege of listening to the Holy Spirit as we do pray. This isn't all up to us. No wonder Paul calls us in Ephesians 6 to pray *"in the Spirit."*

Keep Prayer God-Centered Rather Than Problem-Centered

This is why starting prayer with praise is so important. For a season in my life I found myself avoiding extended prayer because I didn't have the emotional energy to revisit all the discouraging circumstances and situations that needed prayer. My focus was

> **Great intercessors often spend more time adoring God than asking Him for help.**

on the greatness of the problems rather than the greatness of God. I would finish a half hour of prayer more depressed than when I started. But prevailing intercession focuses on God's promises and provision, by faith, more than it concentrates on the overwhelming need. Great intercessors often spend more time adoring God than asking Him for help.

Blend Specific Requests with Spiritual Travail

It's good to keep a prayer list and have a prayer journal to record specific requests and answers. James 4:2 reminds us that the lack of specific answers is often the result of overly generalized praying. However, intercession sometimes takes us past prayer-list praying and into heart-gripping encounters with the grief, passion, and love of God's heart. Interceding in tongues, weeping, and even groaning in spiritual travail may be a part of this. We need to be open, praying through to God's heart and allowing His Spirit to pray God's heart through us. At this point in intercession for others, we may also find ourselves actually pushing back against demonic powers and their purposes as they have attached themselves to the people and situations we are praying for.

Form a Team of Prayer Partners

Paul exhorted the Ephesians to pray at all times "for all the Lord's people," and then he included himself: *"And pray for me"* (Eph. 6:19). I sometimes tell people that I pray for myself just in case no one else is! But how powerful it is when other people are praying specifically for us as well. We need this type of prayer if we are to prevail as ministry leaders. I've often felt buoyed up in my spirit when I should have been pulled down by circumstances and spiritual battles, simply because intercessors were praying for me and God was answering them on my behalf.

At two of the churches I pastored there were about a hundred men in each who committed to be my personal prayer partners. They chose a day of the week (other than Sunday) to specifically pray for me as their pastor. I would send them a personal, a family, and a ministry prayer request for each week. Then on Sundays, teams of men would pray through the Sunday morning services in another room—for me, for the church, and for each other. The teams were organized around the day of the week they had committed to pray for me—the Monday guys on one Sunday, the Tuesday guys the next Sunday, etc. The spin-off was that men learned to pray and even gained the confidence they needed to lead their families spiritually. Meanwhile, I was covered in prayer as a pastor.

P-R-A-Y

Of course, praying for each other is ultimately the task of the whole church. Beyond ministry systems and strategies, this is what makes us strong. So as a way of teaching prayer to everyone, I developed a simple acrostic around the word **P-R-A-Y**. It builds on the example of Nehemiah in the Old Testament. When Nehemiah heard that the walls of Jerusalem were broken down and its gates burned with fire, he wept and fasted for days. The essence of his prayer, as recorded in Nehemiah 1:5–11, follows an intercessory pattern that is easy to learn:

P—Praise

Nehemiah didn't begin his prayer with a request but with an expression of praise. In doing so, he focused on those attributes of God that he would need if the walls were to be rebuilt. He started with the dimensions of God's greatness rather than the dimensions of the challenge.

R—Repent

Approaching God's presence inevitably makes us aware of our own sinfulness and unworthiness. Yet repentance clears out the spiritual clutter and, in the words of John the Baptist, prepares "the way of the Lord." So Nehemiah confessed both his own sins as well as those of his nation.

A—Ask

Prayer isn't twisting the arm of a reluctant God, but touching the heart of a willing God. Nehemiah made his request for rebuilt walls by appealing to God's promises. God's promises express God's willingness. Nehemiah quoted God's Word, stood on God's promises, and, in doing so, humbly asked for God's intervention and help.

Y—Yield

Nehemiah knew that sometimes the Lord calls us to be the answer to our own prayers. He touchingly closed his prayer by personally surrendering to God's purposes and yielding to God's strength. Rather than saying amen, he simply said yes to God's favor, direction, and help.

SPIRITUAL PREVAILING

Grass On Our Path

Intercessory prayer *"for all the saints"* is incredibly potent. It changes ministries and helps us prevail as spiritual communities. The Enemy fights it with every kind of distraction and obstruction he can throw at us, but God honors faith-filled praying.

At the 2010 Lausanne III conference in South Africa, a Pentecostal pastor from Kenya told the story of the East African revival of over fifty years ago. During that time, people would walk well-worn pathways to prayer huts and places of intercession in the forest. When Christians slipped away from prayer, their friends would notice by the condition of their paths, and gently encourage each other: "Brother, the grass grows on your path."[48]

As leaders of God's people, engaged in spiritual battle and committed to prevailing, our challenge is to never let the grass grow on our pathway to prayer.

ENDNOTES

1. http://www.brainyquote.com/quotes/keywords/overnight_success.html
2. Chuck Miller, *The Spiritual Formation of Leaders* (New York: Xulon Press, 2007), 5.
3. James S. Stewart, *The Life and Teaching of Jesus Christ* (Nashville: Abingdon Press, 1978), 24.
4. Eugene H. Peterson, *The Jesus Way* (Grand Rapids: Wm. B. Eerdmans Publishing Co., 2007), 230.
5. Tim Elmore, *Habitudes Book #1: The Art of Self-Leadership, Faith Based* (New York: Tower Books, Poet Gardener, 2010).
6. Frank Bartleman, *Azusa Street* (New Kensington, PA: Whitaker House, 1982), 58.
7. Miles Stanford, *Principles of Spiritual Growth* (Lincoln, NB: Back to the Bible Publisher, 1982).
8. Adapted, in part, from Dick and Ruth Foth, *When the Giant Lies Down* (Wheaton, IL: Victor Books, 1995), 13.
9. J. Oswald Sanders, *Spiritual Leadership* (Chicago: Moody Press, 1989), 20.
10. Bernie May, *Learning to Trust: Developing Confidence in God* (Colorado Springs: Multnomah Publishers, Inc., 1985).
11. www.brainyquote.com/quotes/quotes/p/phillipsbr121609.html
12. Sanders, *Spiritual Leadership*, 21.
13. Robert E. Coleman, *The Master Plan of Evangelism* (Old Tappan, NJ: Spire Books, 1963), 21.
14. Oswald J. Smith, *The Cry of the World* (Great Britain: Purnell and Sons, Ltd., 1959), 47.
15. http://www.crustore.org/fourlawseng.htm
16. Adapted, in part, from Norman Shawchuck and Roger Heuser, *Managing the Congregation*, (Nashville: Abingdon Press, 1996), 43-55.
17. Shawchuck and Heuser, *Managing the Congregation*, 43-55.
18. Brief overview: en.wikipedia.org/wiki/Edwin_Friedman
19. http://lc3.littlechute.k12.wi.us/literacy/Gradual%20Release%20of%20Responsibility.pdf
20. Patrick Lencioni, *Death by Meeting* (San Francisco: Jossey-Bass, 2004).
21. William Manchester, *The Last Lion* (Canada: Little, Brown & Company, 1988), 210.
22. Ibid.
23. Rick Warren, *Preaching for Life Change Seminar Notebook*, 21.
24. http://thinkexist.com/quotation/things_which_matter_most_must_never_be_at_the/180010.html

25. http://en.wikipedia.org/wiki/Edwin_Friedman
26. J. Russell Crabtree, *The Fly in the Ointment* (New York: Church Publishing, 2008), 9.
27. Stephen M. R. Covey, *The Speed of Trust* (New York: Free Press, Simon and Schuster, Inc., 2006), 1.
28. Bob Wells, "Which Way to Clergy Health?" *Divinity*, Fall 2002.
29. Barbara Brown Taylor, "Divine Subtraction," *The Christian Century*, November, 1999.
30. Mayo Clinic online, http://www.mayoclinic.org/diseases-conditions/obesity/basics/causes/con-20014834
31. Todd Ferguson, "Occupational Conditions, Self-Care, and Obesity Among Clergy in the United States," *Journal of Social Science Research*, Volume 49, January 2015, also accessible at http://www.sciencedirect.com/science/article/pii/S0049089X14001690
32. Ibid.
33. Ibid.
34. Mayo Clinic online, http://www.sciencedaily.com/articles/p/physical_exercise.htm.
35. Emily Lenneville, "Why Do I Think Better After I Exercise?" *Scientific American Mind*, Volume 24, Issue 3, June 6, 2013 also accessible at http://www.scientificamerican.com/article/why-do-you-think-better-after-walk-exercise/.
36. Barbara Robb, "Exercise and Physical Activity: What's the Difference?"; Cox Health online, http://www.everydayhealth.com/fitness/basics/difference-between-exercise-and-physical-activity.aspx.
37. Ronald Chernow, *Washington: A Life* (New York: The Penguin Press, 2010), 259.
38. Bill Hybels, "Reading Your Gauges," *Christianity Today: Leadership Journal*, Spring, 1991, 32.
39. Richard A. Swenson, MD, *Margin: Restoring Emotional, Physical, Financial, and Time Reserves to Overloaded Lives* (Colorado Springs: NavPress, 1992), 91–92.
40. Ibid, 103.
41. Fil Anderson, *Running on Empty* (Colorado Springs: WaterBrook Press, 2004), 11, 37.
42. Paula Rinehart, "Good Enough: Are You Trying to Measure Up?" (The Ooze, August 28, 2002), accessible at http://theooze.annex.net/articles/print.cfm?id=101&process=pdf.
43. George Grant, "Unstring the Bow" (King's Meadow Study Center, June 16, 2012) http://kingsmeadow.com/grantianflorilegium/unstring-the-bow/
44. Keith W. Sehnert, M.D., *Stress/Unstress* (Nashville: Augsburg Publishing House, 1981), 38–42.
45. Margaret J. Marcuson, *Leaders Who Last* (New York: Seabury Books, 2009), 3–4.
46. http://www.tentmaker.org/Quotes/prayerquotes3.htm
47. As quoted by Max Anders, *Holman New Testament Commentary–Galatians, Ephesians, Philippians, Colossians* (Nashville: Broadman and Holman Publishers, 1999).
48. James Stuart Bell, *The One Year Men of the Bible: 365 Meditations* (Wheaton, IL: Tyndale House Publishers, 2008), March 6 devotional.

ACKNOWLEDGMENTS

"I thank my God every time I remember you."
PHILIPPIANS 1:3

Having been trained to be an engineer and not a pastor, I have had to primarily rely on the classroom of experience to learn ministry leadership—and a learner I remain to this day. For that reason I feel especially indebted to the family members, mentors, ministry associates, congregations, and friends the Lord has put into my life along the way to help shape and quantify those learning experiences.

My parents, Ted and Rheta Bradford, were not pastors, but they were some of the most active volunteer leaders that I've ever encountered in the local church. My original intention to be a Jesus-loving engineer was predicated, in part, on a conviction gleaned from them that I didn't have to be a pastor to be a minister.

After three years of being a full-time pastor and a single man, the Lord brought my wife, Sandi, into my life. Her father, Paul Lowenberg, was a powerful preacher; her mother was a saint in every way. With those strong ministry influences in her background, as well as her own ministry experiences in the United States and Europe, Sandi's counsel, perspective, and partnership became God's gift to me. She is still my best friend and closest prayer partner. Her brother, Doug Lowenberg, also became a great friend and role model.

Sandi is also a wonderful mom. With her help our two daughters, Meredith and Angeline, have been willing to make huge changes in location and life simply because of

SPIRITUAL PREVAILING

Christ's calling on our family. The Lord has used Meredith and Angeline to make a difference wherever we have been. They are a delight to my heart.

Early in my leadership journey, Dr. George Wood, now General Superintendent of the General Council of the Assemblies of God, became a trusted friend and mentor. One of the most stretching ministry experiences of my life was to follow his seventeen-year tenure as pastor of Newport Mesa Christian Center in the heart of Orange County, California. Since that time he has been instrumental in opening to me many other doors of ministry and service, each one further shaping and forming me as a ministry leader.

My earliest leadership experiences were as a student leader in university ministry. I will never forget the providential influence of a student, friend, and discipler, Duane Flemming; the encouragement and mentoring of national Chi Alpha directors Dave Gable and Dennis Gaylor; and the influence of gifted campus ministry leaders from across the country whose lives and ministry models so imprinted my life.

I also feel deeply indebted to the wonderful associate pastors, staff personnel, board members, and volunteer leaders the Lord gave me the privilege of working with over the past three decades. They are, to this day, people of immense talent and dedication. They are too numerous to name, but so much of what is in this book is the product of life lived and ministry learned together with them.

Partnership with those ministry associates was ultimately made possible by four wonderful church congregations who opened their hearts to me and trusted me to be their pastor—Christians in Action University Church (now Sojourn Campus Church) in Minneapolis, Minnesota; Newport Mesa Christian Center (now Newport Mesa Church) in Costa Mesa, California; Broadway Church in Vancouver, British Columbia; and Central Assembly of God in Springfield, Missouri. Each of these communities of believers invested transformationally in my development as a ministry leader.

I am also indebted to Dr. Byron Klaus for the friend and

influence that he has been in my life. For sixteen years he served as the president of The Assemblies of God Theological Seminary in Springfield, Missouri. No one could have better embodied the seminary's moniker, "Knowledge on Fire." I am, indeed, honored that he would write the foreword to this book.

Finally, let me thank Esther Wood, my executive administrative assistant, for helping me to clear extra time to write over these past few months; Steve and Susan Blount, Vice Presidents of My Healthy Church publishing and marketing, for their enthusiasm over this project; and Terri Gibbs, managing book editor, for her exceptional editorial assistance.

ABOUT THE AUTHOR

Dr. James T. Bradford is the general secretary of the Assemblies of God. Prior to his election as general secretary in 2009, Bradford served as senior pastor of Central Assembly in Springfield, Missouri.

Jim holds a PhD in aerospace engineering from the University of Minnesota. As a student he led a small Chi Alpha campus Bible study that eventually grew into a university church. Upon graduation in 1979, Jim stepped into full-time ministry with that campus outreach. In 1988, Jim and his family moved to southern California where he pastored Newport-Mesa Christian Center in the heart of Orange County.

Twelve years later, he transitioned to Vancouver, BC, to pastor Broadway Church. In 2003 Jim and his family moved to Springfield to assume the pastorate of Central Assembly.

Bradford has also served on a variety of executive boards including that of Vanguard University, the Southern California District Executive Presbytery, Evangel University, and the General Presbytery of the Assemblies of God.

Bradford and his wife, Sandi, have two daughters, Meredith and Angeline.

For More Information

For more information about this and other valuable resources please visit www.salubrisresources.com